An ACCOUNT of
MURDER, MUTINY & MAYHEM

Concerning the affairs of

THE BLACKEST-HEARTED VILLAINS FROM IRISH HISTORY

By the noted chronicler

Joe O'Shea

THE O'BRIEN PRESS
DUBLIN

Photo: Alex Sapienza

JOE O'SHEA is a journalist and broadcaster, originally from Cork, but living and working in Dublin. He has been writing for a range of national newspapers and broadcast media since he was nineteen, first as a news reporter and then as a feature writer, columnist and TV presenter.

DEDICATION

For Holly & Norma

ACKNOWLEDGEMENTS

My friends and family have had to listen to me tell these stories, sometimes repeatedly, over the years and while they have done a very good job in always at least feigning interest, I suspect their constant exhortations to commit my many tales to print were partly in the hope that they would never have to listen to them again.

So I have to say thanks to my brother, Ken, sisters, Niamh and Jennifer, my mother, Norma, and to Holly, who always said there should be space on our bookshelves for at least one book with my name on it.

Also, I'd probably still be talking about the book if it wasn't for the kind advice, encouragement and prompting of the author Des Ekin, who sat listening to me rave about cannibalism and whiskey over a cup of coffee and pointed me in the general direction of The O'Brien Press. Thanks also to Mary, Michael, my editor, Helen, and all the staff at The O'Brien Press who have always encouraged, helped and shown the kind of light touch which, at first, proved to be confusing for a veteran of twenty years in the newspaper business.

And lastly, with stories covering such a wide swathe of history, so many locations and so many different individuals and events, it would have been impossible to even start without the work of so many people, historians, journalists, correspondents and chroniclers, who went before. Hopefully, I have acknowledged at least some of them in the references.

First published 2012 by
The O'Brien Press Ltd,
12 Terenure Road East, Rathgar,
Dublin 6, Ireland.
Tel: +353 1 4923333; Fax: +353 1 4922777
E-mail: books@obrien.ie.
Website: www.obrien.ie
ISBN: 978-1-84717-299-0
Text © copyright Joe O'Shea 2012
Copyright for typesetting, layout, editing, design
© The O'Brien Press Ltd

Printed and bound by CPI Group (UK) Ltd, Croydon, CR0 4YY
The paper used in this book is produced using pulp from managed forests

Picture Credits:
Picture section: P1 James 'Sligo' Jameson; p4, centre, Sir Hugh Gough; p4, bottom Alejandro O'Reilly; p6, bottom, Dr Knox; p7, bottom, Thomas Meagher all © The Bridgeman Art Library. P2, top, The Stanley Expedition; p2, bottom, Thomas Heazle-Parke; p4, top, Dom Pedro; p5 Battle of Sobraon; p6, top, William Burke; p7, top, William Hare; all © Mary Evans Picture Library. P3, top, Walsh Coat of Arms; used by kind permission of Eddie Geoghegan. P3, bottom, Chateau de Serrant; used by kind permission of Country Life. P8, top & bottom, Vincent Coll © Getty Images.

FOREWORD

Like many Irish schoolboys of my generation, I got a solid, no-non-
sense education from the Christian Brothers, robust men steeped
in the heroic tradition of Irish history. We learned about Michael
Collins, Daniel O'Connell, Robert Emmet, Hugh O'Neill, the
Kennedys and Brian Boru. At home we had books by Old IRA
men such as Tom Barry and Dan Breen and heard stories of the
burning of Cork (my home town) by the hated Black and Tans,
during which a grand-aunt of mine was killed by a stray bullet
while she sat over her sewing in her front room.

These men were stern, square-jawed patriots who subsisted on
black tea and rough bread, marched for days across rocky mountains and knelt to say their prayers before going into battle for
Irish freedom. We were told how the Irish, either as missionaries,
scholars or soldiers had scattered to the four corners of the world,
bringing the light of learning or of freedom to benighted people
everywhere. It was stirring stuff. But something was always missing. Where were the bad guys?

A life-long passion, bordering on obsession, for history – and
especially the stories of Irish mavericks and renegades – brought
rumours of Irish men who were not so noble, learned or Christian. I collected them through the years, the forgotten or ignored
stories of the Irish slavers, mercenaries, pirates, killers, cheats and
madmen. In many cases, their stories are only shadows thrown
across the pages of other people's histories. You find a thread, a

mention of an Irish name or place, and pull at it, hoping to find out more.

In this way I found out about the two-and-a-half-thousand Munster farmers who took a wrong turn and ended up burning Rio de Janeiro, the Donegal-born gangster that even the New York Mafia feared and the Meathman who ruled New Orleans for the Spanish with an iron fist in a mailed-glove.

Some of these accounts are shocking, others almost unbelievable, and a few border on the wilder dreams of the most addled Hollywood scriptwriter. But I hope that all of them are interesting and even, in some cases at least, fun. After all, what is history without the bad guys?

CONTENTS

James 'Sligo' Jameson
— The Whiskey Cannibal and the Heart of Darkness.

In a jungle clearing in an unmapped region of the Congo River basin, an Irish gentleman discusses the rites and rituals of cannibalism with a slave trader. James 'Sligo' Jameson, scion of the famous whiskey-distilling family and one of the great naturalists of the late-nineteenth-century 'age of exploration', is far from home, fever-wracked and travelling under the dubious protection of the notorious Arab slave master, Tippu Tib.

Jameson is a well-bred, very well-connected Victorian gentleman-explorer famed for his sketches of butterflies and birds, made during previous travels through Southern Africa, Borneo and the Rocky Mountains of the North America continent; he's hardy and ready to face danger in the previously-impenetrable Ituri forest of the Congo basin. He has been fascinated with science and nature since he began collecting birds' eggs around the family home at Glen Lodge, Co. Sligo as a young boy. But in April 1888, he is hopelessly lost, cut adrift from the main column, abandoned by the legendary explorer who recruited him to take part in the greatest expedition of the age, Henry Morton Stanley.

Struggling along a slavers' trail towards the village of Kasongo, a reluctant, desperate guest of Tippu Tib — independent Arab warlord and trader — and his private army, Jameson has, between bouts of fever, been nursing a dark and growing fascination with stories of cannibalism. The only other white officer in the rag-tag column, British Army Major Edmund Musgrave Barttelot, is going slowly mad. Barttelot has already kicked one camp boy to death and killed another with three hundred lashes from a rhino-hide bullwhip. He will shortly be shot dead by a local gang-master after physically attacking the man's wife.

Bivouacked overnight in a jungle clearing, Jameson once again pesters his host about the 'travellers' tales' he has heard concerning the local tribes and the butchery and eating of slaves. This time, perhaps annoyed by his guest's obsession with cannibalism, Tippu Tib offers a practical demonstration.

What happened next would be at the centre of the final, gruesome chapter of the story of the heroic age of European exploration in Africa and its enduring legacy of brutal con-quest, instability and exploitation. It would pit Henry Morton Stanley, the journalist and adventurer who found fame as 'the man who found Dr Livingstone' against the Jameson family and become one of the great international scandals of the late-Victorian era. Allegations and counter-allegations made by Stanley, survivors of the expedition, the Jameson family and British colonial officials would be made via letters and editorials in the most influ-ential newspapers of Dublin, London and New York. Stanley and his allies would accuse Jameson of the most horrible crime, buying a young slave girl for the 'sole purpose of having her murdered, so that a cannibalistic scene might be furnished for his sketch book'.

The Jameson family would accuse Stanley and others of fabricating horror stories and attacking the reputation of an honourable man who could not defend himself. Stanley's expedition had become a three-year, continent-crossing trek of slaughter, savagery and disease, costing thousands of lives, and attracting fierce public criticism; the great man would be accused of finding a convenient fall-guy in Jameson.

What would never be in question was the fact that a father and husband, who had dreamed of exploring Africa as a young boy, poring over maps in his grandmother's house in Co. Sligo, met a terrible, squalid end in a disease-ridden camp.

The scandal would drag on for years and the Jameson name, for a time, became synonymous not with whiskey, but with cannibalism; there is even strong evidence that James 'Sligo' Jameson was the model for Joseph Conrad's Mr Kurtz in his classic story of civilisation, madness and the Congo, *Heart of Darkness*.

Conrad, the Polish-seafarer-turned-British-novelist had only recently returned from his time as a river boat captain in the Congo when the press was full of accounts of the appalling behaviour of Stanley's officers on his last, disastrous expedition. Conrad's biographer Chris Fletcher cites the infamous, real-life, tale of the Irish gentleman naturalist who consorted with cannibals and notes the great novelist described Mr Kurtz starting out as 'an emissary of pity, and science, and progress'. Conrad has Kurtz 'presiding at certain midnight dances ending up with unspeakable rites, which ... were offered up to him – do you understand? – to Mr Kurtz himself.' These words eerily mirror the charges laid against James Sligo Jameson.

Further parallels may be seen when Conrad writes of Kurtz's widow and her inability to deal with the truth of her late husband's madness. However, Conrad, Ethel Jameson and the readers of the Victorian press might never have learned the true story of James 'Sligo' Jameson if it wasn't for a few survivors, including a Roscommon-born doctor and adventurer, who miraculously survived a cross-continental trek of almost unimaginable horror and difficulty. Their story and the true motives for what has become known as 'The Last Expedition', reveal the darkness at the heart of the great age of exploration in Africa.

That the gentle, butterfly-obsessed grandson of a Dublin distiller should have been there at all is one of those strange quirks of history, a forgotten chapter in the story of an Irish family name known throughout the world. It involves ruthless newspaper magnates in New York and London, a rapacious Belgian king, private African armies, renegades, slave traders, corrupt politicians and a famous explorer with a secret past. And it begins with the one of the most dramatic convulsions of the High Victorian age, the killing of Major-General Charles George Gordon at Khartoum.

★ ★ ★

On 10 December 1886, the prominent Scottish doctor Robert Felkin wrote a letter to the *Times,* calling the attention of all patriotic Britishers to the plight of one 'Dr Mehemet Emim', one of the few survivors of the fall of Khartoum in January of the previous year.

Khartoum had been a traumatic event for the British empire. The revered, legendary soldier and adventurer General Charles George Gordon had found himself at the sharp end of a complicated power-play involving British political factions, the Empire's client ruler in Egypt (the Khedive) and a self-anointed Islamic warrior-messiah, the Mahdi Muhammad Ahmad. Starting in 1881, the 'Mad Mahdi' as he was dubbed by the British press, swept through Egyptian territory in the Sudan with a huge army, slaughtering Egyptian garrisons and threatening the strategic Blue Nile city of Khartoum and lower Egypt itself.

The then British Prime Minister, William Gladstone, wanted no involvement in further imperial adventures in the Sudan. But powerful interests in Britain, backed by a popular, jingoistic press who loudly supported British interests abroad, wanted to expand the empire and put a halt to the threat of Islamic fundamentalists driving towards the strategically vital Suez Canal, the 'Highway to India'.

The British, through their Consul General in Egypt, Sir Evelyn Baring (known in Cairo as 'Over-Baring' thanks to his bullying approach to the natives) instructed the Egyptians to evacuate their garrisons far up on the Blue Nile. General Gordon was despatched to pull out the seven thousand Egyptian troops and many thousands more civilians. But the maverick soldier, popularly known as 'Chinese Gordon' after his adventures in the Far East, had other ideas.

On reaching Khartoum on 18 February 1884, the General, who firmly believed that Britain should stop the Mahdi in his tracks, immediately disregarded his promise (and clear orders) to evacuate and instead set about organising the defence of the city. What followed was a game of nerves, involving Gladstone and the anti-war party in London, the jingoists in Britain and Egypt, and the two men at the centre of the story, the Mahdi and Gordon.

Gordon apparently believed he could hold at Khartoum long enough to shame Gladstone into sending the military assistance needed to defeat the Islamic army camped outside. All sides were playing for time and Gordon lost. While a relief expedition was very slowly making its way to Khartoum, the Mahdi's fifty-thou-sand-strong army burst through the defences on the night of 25 January and slaughtered the thousands of soldiers and civilians who had not already starved to death.

Gordon was amongst those killed, either making a heroic last stand or trying to escape, depending on which account you believe. And the huge public outcry in Britain, which included a leaked telegram of admonishment from Queen Victoria to her Prime Minister, resulted in the fall of the government.

Meanwhile, to the South of Khartoum, an enigmatic figure known as Emin Pasha was now effectively the outside world's last man standing in the region.

Emin Pasha was one of those extraordinary men thrown up

by the fluid, rapidly-shifting political landscape in Europe and in the lands nominally controlled by the Turkish Ottoman Empire towards the end of the nineteenth century.

Born into a German-Jewish family in the Oppelen region of upper Silesia (today, Opole in Poland) in 1840, the boy born Isaak Eduard Schnitzer, would travel from Silesia to central Africa via Albania, Turkey and Egypt, going from the Jewish to the Lutheran to the Islamic religion on that journey.

He was a brilliant linguist and administrator, with a knack for self-preservation and a nose for impending trouble.

Emin Pasha was the governor of the Egyptian province of Equatoria (in Southern Sudan) on the Upper Nile (in reality, some few thousand soldiers and their families in dusty outposts) when Khartoum fell. Realising that his benefactor, Gordon, was gone and the escape route to the north was cut off with no prospect of help, he gathered his soldiers, their women and children and headed south, deeper into the heart of Africa through Congo and Uganda.

Emin Pasha had effectively been cut loose as a free agent by his British and Egyptian masters. He still had his own small army, but it was up to him to carve out a safe haven for his people amidst constantly-warring kingdoms, rapacious slave traders and the general chaos of the vast, uncharted region. In one respect he was fortunate. His connection to Gordon, and the interests of British missionaries and empire-builders with their eyes on the immense and unclaimed Congo region, made him a valuable asset.

'Emin Pasha is the noblest of Gordon's lieutenants,' wrote the Scottish doctor and friend of missionaries Robert Felkin to the *Times* in December 1886. 'To remove [him] would be to deliver his province once more to barbarism and the slaver; to maintain him where he is and give him adequate support would be to plant a broad area of civilisation in the very heart of Africa.' Felkin's letter had a galvanising effect; in late 1886, the cry was raised by the *Times* of London; 'We Must Save Emin Pasha!'

Meanwhile in Africa, a Scottish missionary and empire enthusiast called Alexander Mackay, who had been in Uganda for many years and met with Emin Pasha when he came south, had managed to get word through to the British consul in Zanzibar. Mackay communicated to Emin Pasha the need to stoke public opinion in London and force the hand of the British Government.

'The old Government in Khartoum no longer exists,' Mackay wrote to Emin, 'but you can deliver over a large territory to English hands, if you wish to do so. A good Governor such as you are should take over the whole territory of the Nile sources, I know quite well that you could bring all this about if you took it in hand. You must, however, be supported and England will without doubt help you if you say so.'

The consul-general in Zanzibar, Frederick Holmwood, alerted to the 'plight of Christian men and loyal Egyptians', cabled London on their behalf. 'News from Uganda, 12 July [1886], Terrible persecution broken out, all native Christians being put to death. Missionaries in extreme danger; Emin at Wadelai holds province, but urgently needs ammunition and stores. Objects if he can avoid it, deserting the four thousand loyal Egyptian subjects there. No time to be lost if assistance decided on.'

Further dispatches, distributed via missionaries and anti-slavery groups across Britain and the continent, and eagerly published by the newspapers, continued to stoke the flames of public opinion. Emin Pasha himself wrote in a letter: 'I remain here the last and only representative of Gordon's staff. It therefore falls to me, and is my bounden duty, to follow up the road he showed us. Sooner or later a bright future must be drawn for these countries, sooner or later these people will be drawn into the circle of the ever advancing civilised world.'

The memory of Gordon's heroic stand in Khartoum and the national shame felt at the failure to help him was still very fresh in the minds of the public. And now here was another loyal servant of the empire (albeit one with a foreign-sounding name) trapped in deepest, darkest Africa, surrounded by savages, yet bravely clinging on to Christianity, civilisation, Queen and Empire. Here was a chance to avenge the fallen hero, erase the shame of Khartoum and save Emin Pasha and his brave band of loyal subjects.

Except, of course, the British Government wanted nothing to do with yet another hugely-expensive military campaign (the failed mission to rescue Gordon had cost £11.5m) into the uncharted heart of Africa to rescue a man they considered a German subject turned servant of the Egyptians. But what Government could or would not do, private enterprise and the greatest explorers of the day could achieve.

Another Scotsman, William Mackinnon, had made his fortune as one of the partners in the British East India Steam Navigation Company (one of his biggest revenue streams came from transporting Empire troops to far-flung outposts in Africa and India). A religious man, committed to supporting missionary work and the abolition of the slave trade (then still ravaging central Africa), Mackinnon recognised a golden opportunity when he saw one.

A relief expedition would save Emin Pasha, open up the region to British missionaries and traders and would almost certainly see Central East Africa come under the direct rule of the still expanding empire, a development that would be good for businessmen in various areas, such as, say, the troop-carrying trade. And if Mackinnon dreamt big, he could even see himself and his associates as the rulers of their own, private kingdom in East Africa. It had been done before.

The Scotsman became the driving force behind the Emin Pasha Relief Committee, newly set up to organise an expedition to go in and save Gordon's former associate. Mackinnon contacted Henry Morton Stanley, the world-famous explorer and old Congo hand, who agreed to postpone a lecture tour of the US to return to England.

Stanley had found worldwide fame as the journalist and explorer who had found Doctor David Livingstone, crossing the continent of Africa to the shores of Lake Tanganyika in 1871 and uttering the immortal line, 'Dr Livingstone, I presume?'

The illegitimate son of a teenage domestic servant and (it was rumoured) the local solicitor in a small Welsh town, Stanley had grown up in a workhouse from the age of six before leaving for America to reinvent himself. He was said to have fought on both sides of the US Civil War before becoming a brilliant – some would say brilliantly self-promoting – foreign correspondent for the *New York Herald* newspaper.

Stanley also had links to King Leopold II of Belgium, working for him as a development agent in the King's privately-owned commercial holdings, the Congo Free State. The King's vast holdings were massively profitable, but a by-word for terrible exploitation and slavery (which would be later exposed to the world by the pioneering Irish humanitarian campaigner Roger Casement).

Mackinnon and his business associates had plans for a similar commercial venture in East Africa. Their proposal, to be carried by Stanley to Emin Pasha, was for the former Governor to be set up in a well-paid job overseeing a vast commercial enterprise, free from the interference of the British and other governments. If they could pull it off, they would be masters of a huge tract of Africa and its resources, with the tacit backing of the British Empire. The land might nominally be in the name of a puppet chief, or simply 'administered' as a commercial enterprise with a Royal charter (for the benefit, education and salvation of the 'natives', of course) before eventually becoming a dominion of the British crown, as vast tracts of Africa and the Indian sub-continent had before.

Naturally, the public at large didn't need to know about the details. The Emin Pasha Relief Expedition would be portrayed as a mission of mercy to save the Pasha and his people, protect missionaries and set up a British-allied state that would act as a check to the armies of the Mahdi, which were still a threat despite his demise from disease in the year after the fall of Khartoum.

For Stanley, it would be one last glorious hurrah, securing a well-paid future of fame, best-selling accounts of adventures amongst the 'savages' and lecture tours. All who travelled with him would have to sign a document promising not to publish any account of the expedition until at least six months after his own came out (and he already had a title: *In Darkest Africa*).

Stanley's previous expedition to the Congo, described by himself in the best-seller *How I Found Livingstone,* had been controversial, with accusations of poor judgement, reckless treatment of colleagues and the brutal beating of bearers. This new expedition would shake off this taint and would be the largest, best-funded and best-equipped (in terms of manpower, talent and resources) ever mounted in Africa. The Welsh-born adventurer secured the backing of powerful US and British commercial interests, including newspapers eager for tales of heroism from faraway places, and set up in London to recruit his people in late 1886.

Amongst the ex-soldiers, would-be adventurers and colonial rough-necks there would be a small cadre of 'gentleman volunteers' – the first of which was James 'Sligo' Jameson. He was one of over four hundred men who applied to join the expedition, which he saw as an unrivalled opportunity to examine the flora and fauna of a region virtually unexplored by Europeans.

Jameson was a talented, well-travelled artist and naturalist. His drawings of birds and butterflies made in Africa, Borneo, Ceylon and in the heart of the continental US greatly impressed Stanley (although the explorer warned Jameson that there might not be much time for water-colours where they were going). Jameson was also rich enough to offer to volunteer, and make a donation of £1,000 to the relief committee.

However, Stanley was concerned about the thirty-one-year-old Jameson's physical frailty. The naturalist assured him that a life spent travelling the world in the service of science (which started with him using ladders to climb up some cliffs and observe nesting birds in Sligo) had made him hardier than he seemed. It is not known whether Stanley realised that Jameson was married with a family, a factor that might have dissuaded the explorer from taking him on; Jameson had married Ethel Durand in 1885 and they had two children, Ethel Gladys (who died in 1933) and Algernon, who was born after his father had left for Africa and lived until 1965.

Jameson was unaware of the confidential commercial objectives of the expedition's backers. And as plans were being finalised in London, Henry Morton Stanley was in communication with his old boss King Leopold, who dropped something of a bombshell.

The King wrote to the committee, pointing out that as Stanley was still contracted in his service, he could not release him for the Emin Pasha relief *unless* the expedition travelled from west to east across his lands in the Congo, and not from east to west, considered the safer, shorter and more direct route. Mackinnon and the commercial backers of the relief expedition had wanted their man to go through the virgin territory they wanted to annexe. They had been outmanoeuvred.

The committee was forced to completely change its plans. For the expedition, it meant a far greater trek through much more dangerous territory.

For King Leopold, it meant the chance to vastly expand his own private empire. Stanley slipped away to Brussels to confer with the king and get his instructions; on behalf of the king, Stanley would make the same offer to Emin Pasha that the Scots empire-builder Mackinnon was considering. King Leopold would annexe the territory into the Congo Free State and Emin Pasha would be placed on a large salary to administrate it for him. Stanley was playing both sides, accepting the backing of the British while promising his old employer the King of Belgium a favourable outcome. Leopold was confident that once his experienced African troops and administrators were in place in the new territories, Mackinnon would have to back off.

With these machinations going on in the background, the European contingent of the expedition finally set sail from England on 20 January 1887. They were laden down with stores, arms and ammunition and trade goods, which included fifteen miles of cloth, two tonnes of beads and one tonne of wire (all for trading). They also had two tonnes of gunpowder, rifles, hundreds of thousands of rounds of ammunition and newly-developed Maxim machine gun, personally donated by its inventor Sir Hiram Maxim. Every single ounce of stores, goods and ammunition would have to be carried for thousands of miles through terrible, uncharted terrain by an army of local bearers.

During a stopover in Cairo, Stanley also took on a twenty-nine-year-old Irish doctor serving with the British Military, Dr Thomas Heazle Parke, as the expedition's medical officer. Dr Parke, born in Kilmore, Co. Roscommon in 1857 and brought up in Carrick-on-Shannon in Co. Leitrim, would play a significant role in the expedition and the subsequent controversy. By any measure, Parke was a remarkable man and if any member of the expedition could have been considered a hero, it was the modest, resolute and kindly Leitrim doctor.

After a further stop in Zanzibar, the expedition proceeded to the mouth of the Congo river via the Cape. At the mouth of the Congo, Stanley was shocked to see a squadron of German warships at anchor where, on his earlier visits, the Royal Navy had been present. It was a highly-visible sign of the 'Scramble for Africa' that was heating up, even as the expedition was touching on African shores.

To get to Emin Pasha, Stanley was realist enough to know that he would have to deal with the ivory and slave merchant Tippu Tib, who controlled the whole region between Lake Tanganyika and the Upper Congo. He knew Tippu Tib could effectively block his efforts to get from the Congo to Lake Albert and the Upper

Nile, where Emin Pasha and his people were awaiting the column, and could also block King Leopold's efforts to expand his private empire to the Upper Nile region.

The politics of the situation were beyond the ken of James 'Sligo' Jameson, but as early as Cape Town he was beginning to realise that his dreams of a great scientific exploration of the Congo might not be in keeping with the more practical aims of Stanley.

His chief's refusal to allow him a personal bearer to carry his collecting apparatus and guns took 'a good deal of the gilt off the trip for me', he noted in his diary at the Cape, adding that he had understood his role to be 'to collect and shoot meat for the expedition'. It was to be a disillusioning journey up the Congo in steamships provided by the King, 'I have never been on a trip where there is so little enjoyment of any kind, it is all so serious,' wrote Jameson. That Jameson was still referring to the expedition as a 'trip' and bemoaning the lack of enjoyment involved, is an indication of just how unprepared he was, at least mentally, for what lay ahead of him.

The expedition soon ran into trouble, the five hundred or so West African bearers were reluctant explorers, and malaria and other forms of exotic diseases (for which the Europeans had little or no effective medicines) hit all involved. Stanley, a brilliant but hard-driving, uncompromising and often brutal man, had no time for the moaning of well-born gentlemen who found themselves struggling through swamp and jungle in conditions that would be daunting even to the most hardened travellers today. Unlike many of the explorers who had gone, often virtually alone, into Africa before them, these gentlemen had paid good money to be part of a well-organised and well-stocked expedition. They expected some hardships, naturally, but there would also be game shooting and sport along the way before they returned home in triumph. Stanley later talked of being driven to distraction by the squabbling and complaining done by some of his more refined colleagues.

Jameson did get to do some collecting and sketching. But as the expedition reached the river staging post of Yambuya on 15 June 1887, Stanley was ready to put into action his plan to split the column, a move that would prove disastrous and deeply controversial.

A 'Rear Column', as the expedition leader called it, would remain in a fortified camp at Yambuya to either await Stanley's return after he had reached Emin Pasha at Lake Albert or follow him on, always providing the had the men, ammunition and supplies, which would be provided by Tippu Tib. It was a dangerously loose plan. Communication in the jungle was almost impossible. Some of those left behind had little to no experience of the region and of dealing with the local warlords, slavers and chieftains. Stanley must have known he was taking a huge risk, but he also knew that he had to hurry and could not let the cumbersome main column slow him down.

Stanley had already had several blazing rows with his second in command, a high-handed British army officer called Major Edmund Musgrave Barttelot, who was showing signs of brutality towards the bearers and camp workers and antipathy towards his chief. Of course, attitudes to African people were very different at the time and some cruelty and much racism was expected, but Barttelot's actions went far beyond what was acceptable even then. He was showing growing signs of madness and even sadism in his brutal treatment of those who were there to carry their loads.

Barttelot, already judged to be unstable by some of the Europeans, would stay behind. In his own letters home, the major recorded his bitter resentment of Stanley and his suspicions (which proved to be entirely well-founded) that his chief would leave him in charge of a hospital camp, containing the sick, the lame and the worst deserters, troublemakers and shirkers.

Stanley would make his eight-hundred mile or so sprint for Lake Albert with the fittest of the men. But he would also leave behind Jameson as a help to the major. Jameson was now under no illusions; two weeks before they reached Yambuya, he had witnessed two of the officers, gentleman volunteer Arthur Jephson (the heir to considerable land holdings in Ireland) and Lieutenant William Stairs get into a blazing row with Stanley over the violent looting of a peaceful native village. Stanley, ever the pragmatist, had warned his officers that burning friendly villages was not the way to get the local people on your side. And they would need their goodwill and help if they were to survive what was now becoming a very perilous situation.

Stanley had already threatened to go on by himself. Barttelot only held back because of his unwavering sense of duty as a British officer. They were far from home, inexperienced, except for their increasingly authoritarian and isolated chief, and homesick. On what was, at home in England, Cup Day at Ascot Races (one of the highlights of high-society's season), Jameson's thoughts turned homewards, writing in his diary; 'I wonder if, amongst the number of one's friends there, any of them will give a thought to those who are absent like myself?'

They were over 1,300 miles from the sea, beyond the last vestige of any 'civilisation' and at Yambuya, two men, Barttelot and Jameson would be effectively abandoned with a few score bearers, dependent on the goodwill and help of the Arab slaver Tippu Tib and the vague promise of further help coming up-river from Leopoldville or back from the forward column.

Stanley was supposed to be gone for five months at the most, dashing off to meet Emin Pasha; he would return to Yambuya to link up once again with Barttelot and his second-in-command Jameson, they would then bring up the bulk of supplies, arms and ammunition to Lake Albert.

The great explorer knew that the Major was probably not up to the job of keeping order and calm in the rear camp, but he confided to Lt Stairs that he hoped the 'experience' of Jameson would hold him in check. Stanley was putting a lot of faith and responsibility in a naturalist he had considered from the start to be frail and not really up to the hard road. Stanley left very detailed instructions for the rear column, covering a wide range of scenarios and all pointing to the conclusion that he did not really expect to be in a position to offer them any further help himself. He would later face accusations of abandoning the column to a deeply uncertain fate.

With Stanley dashing off and the two men facing the reality of long isolation amongst tribes and local warlords whom they could reasonably expect to slit their throats at any moment, Jameson was in mournful mood, 'Alas for all my bright dreams about the march from the [Stanley] Falls to Wadelai,' he wrote.

On the day Stanley departed, the two men found themselves with around a hundred and thirty of the 'very worst sort of wretches', their bearers, including an 'utterly worthless' headman, scant provisions, little chance of game from the exhausted jungle around them and with sickness and disease already stalking the camp.

Stanley marched off into the jungle to face one of the toughest treks in the history of modern exploration, five months of dodging hostile local tribes (including Pygmies who would shoot at them with poisoned arrows), shedding men and officers almost every step of the way and in some cases, effectively abandoning fatally-diseased comrades who threatened to slow him down. These would be left with a bearer and told to hurry back up to the column once they had recovered their strength, an unlikely scenario as all involved must have known.

While making this nightmare trip he was accompanied by

one of the few men, perhaps the only man, who could claim to have come out of the Emin Pasha expedition with his reputation enhanced; Irish doctor, Thomas Heazle Parke, who had volunteered for Stanley after serving with the British army in Egypt (where he was part of the Gordon Relief Expedition to Khartoum), displayed great heroism and resourcefulness, saving the lives of a number of men during a brutal, three-year trek across Africa even though he suffered from terrible bouts of malaria himself. Dr Parke had been close to death himself at one point when a young Pygmy slave-girl who was acting as his servant nursed him back to strength. It was said that Dr Parke formed a strong bond with the girl and had wished to bring her back to 'civilisation'. But she could not or would not leave the forest. At one stage during the final trek to the coast, Dr Parke had himself helped to bring a seriously ill Stanley back from the brink of death, earning the soubriquet 'The Man Who Saved Stanley'.

That was in the future for both men. In the late summer of 1887, the column that had started out as eight hundred men in Zanzibar was down to a starving band of a hundred and fifty when they finally struggled out of the Ituri forest. By the time they reached the shores of Lake Albert on 15 December 1887, it was Stanley and his rag-tag column of skeletons who needed rescuing. It was there that he took a momentous decision, despite not having found Emin Pasha, they would turn back to the highlands above the Lake and try to regroup.

What followed was a long wait for further supplies while the enigmatic Emin Pasha, who in truth, did now not need help, remained elusive. The Pasha had managed to establish himself and his little army in quite a stable mini-kingdom, his emotional, pathetic appeals for help to the British had been made some time before and by the time Stanley staggered into his region, he would have been happy to stay where he was, trading with the locals and the Arabs from the coast and free from the interference of the outside world. Eventually, Emin Pasha heard about this British column and came down from his headquarters by steam boat to meet Stanley on 29 April 1888.

Stanley celebrated the meeting with Emin Pasha with three bottles of champagne that had been carried all of the way up from the mouth of the Congo. Emin Pasha, horrified at the state of the men who had been sent to 'rescue' him, set about feeding and clothing his would-be saviours. On 16 June, Stanley, after strained and inconclusive talks, decided to leave and belatedly turned his attentions to finding the Rear Column, travelling back towards Yambuya.

Emin Pasha, the object of so much effort on the part of Stanley, his men, the British press, the Scottish money-men and the Belgian King, had politely declined to be 'saved' by the starving men in rags.

At Banalya, around ninety-five miles upriver from Yambuya, in mid-August, after almost four months of travel, Stanley ran into William Bonny, a British army sergeant and doctor's assistant on the expedition who had been detached back to the Rear Column, but had arrived at the camp at Yambuya only to find a 'charnel house' (as Stanley later recalled) where he had expected to find the two white officers and their men.

In his subsequent book, Stanley described their meeting, which was conducted with little emotion on his side: 'Well, Bonny, how are you? Where is the Major? Sick, I suppose?'

Bonny replied, 'The Major is dead, sir'.

Bonny had learned that Barttelot had died at the hands of one of the African men after appearing to go mad. On the very day that Stanley and Bonny met, Jameson, who had left for a post further down river in search of help, lay dying at a place called Bangala. The column had not heard from Stanley in over a year. The camp had broken down in utter confusion and violence. Barttelot had been driven mad by the isolation and inactivity. He kicked one small boy to death for a minor infringement and regularly handed out over one-hundred lashes or execution by firing squad to porters who committed crimes as small as falling asleep at their posts.

Jameson, on the other hand, had at first whiled away the long months of isolation with sketching and collecting. He began to hate the bearers, remarking in his diary, 'I think the Zanzibaris are quite the most barefaced liars I have ever met in my life'. He watched their local bearers, barely skeletons, getting over a hundred lashes with a rhino-skin whip, remarking only that they were 'wonderfully plucky' as they 'never uttered a sound' under the lash. Jameson had, by then, decided that exploring was 'nothing but beating niggers with a stick'. Jameson was, by Victorian standards, an educated, well-travelled and relatively-enlightened man. His great passion in life was making delicate watercolours of butterflies. The brutality, isolation and sickness of the Congo was turning him into something else.

By December, scores of the men had died through disease and starvation. On 29 January, Jameson recorded the temperature at Yambuya at over 130 degrees and observed; 'this waiting is sickening. The men are dying off like rotten sheep.'

On 10 August 1888, while making another fruitless journey in search of news from Stanley or from further downriver, Jameson made what would be his last entry in his diary, noting a 'curious scene' when they came upon a band of locals while canoeing along a river in the dark of night. 'All at once it became lit up with dozens of fires on both sides, throwing a bright light back into the forest and across the water. We glided on without a sound from us, but the zip-zip of paddles, drums beating, horns blowing, shouts and cries on every side. I don't think I ever heard such a noise before. We shot out away to our right, and soon left all the tumult behind. What they thought of us I should like to know.'

By the time he reached the expedition camp at Bangala a week later, he was in the final stages of hematuric fever (a form of malarial fever) and about to die in the arms of a white officer who took him, from his canoe, as a 'deathlike figure'. At this stage, Stanley was not much more than a hundred miles away.

Stanley was more outraged than saddened by the terrible end met by both Barttelot and Jameson, he blamed them for being incompetent, weak and for failing to follow his orders. The great explorer had been deeply frustrated by Emin Pasha's unwillingness to be rescued and after further mishaps and bungles, made it to the coast and Zanzibar in late 1889 with a greatly reduced force.

He went to Cairo and wrote the nine-hundred-page account, *In Darkest Africa*, in just fifty days before departing for London and what was, at first, a hero's welcome.

It was two years after the death of Jameson, when Stanley was embroiled in great controversy about the Emin Pasha debacle and needed some ammunition to fire back at his critics, that the strange, disturbing rumours about the Irish gentleman naturalist, James Sligo Jameson, became public. William Bonny, the former British army sergeant who had fallen out with Stanley (the explorer had called his former comrade 'the worst kind of specious rogue') resurfaced, and at the prompting of Stanley recounted the tale first told by another survivor, an interpreter Assad Farad, two years previously. Farad had been at the Yambaya camp with Jameson for two months. He told a shocking tale in which Jameson had bought a young slave girl from Tippu Tib for six handkerchiefs. Farad claimed that Jameson had become fascinated with cannibalism and bought the girl for the express purpose of handing her over to cannibals from the Manyuema tribe. As they slaughtered and prepared the body, Jameson made sketches of the scene.

When Farad, a Syrian, had first made the allegations, the fate of the expedition was still unknown. And while his tales had caused something of a stir, few where willing to take the word of an 'Oriental' over the reputation of a Victorian gentleman; Farad had actually withdrawn the allegations, under pressure from the Emin Pasha Relief Committee. But now Bonny, a white, former British army sergeant was making the same accusations. And the story exploded in the British, American and European newspapers.

The Jameson family were outraged, they accused Bonny of acting on behalf of the increasingly under-fire Stanley (ironically, when Stanley first heard the tales of Jameson's behaviour while in the Congo, he dismissed them as being 'inconceivable nonsense, a sensational *canard*').

Ethel Jameson, the wife of the accused man, thought she could save her husband's reputation by making public his diaries. It was a terrible misjudgement. Incredibly, these diary extracts only served to confirm that the basic facts of the story were true.

Jameson himself wrote of talking to Tippu Tib during a stop on the trail and chiding him about the 'travellers' tales' of cannibalism that most people in Britain considered 'lies'. 'He then said something to an Arab called Ali, seated next to him, who turned around to me and said; "Give me a bit of cloth, and see."'

Jameson then tells what happened next:

'I sent my boy for six handkerchiefs, thinking it was all a joke, and that they were not in earnest, but presently a man appeared, leading a young girl of about ten years old by the hand, and then I witnessed the most horribly sickening sight I am ever likely to see in my life. He plunged a knife quickly into her breast twice, and she fell on her face, turning over on her side. Three men then ran forward, and began to cut up the body of the girl, finally her head was cut off, and not a particle remained, each man taking away his piece down to the river to wash it. The most extraordinary thing was that the girl never uttered a sound, nor struggled, until she fell. Until the last moment I could not believe that they were in earnest. I have heard many stories of this kind since I have been in this country, but never could believe them, and I never would have been such a beast to witness this, but I could not bring myself to believe that it was anything save a rise to get money out of me until the last moment.'

The interpreter, Farad, also told how Jameson drew and sketched throughout the entire ritual. The white man had, he said, later rendered these sketches in six delicate watercolours. The pictures were of the girl being led away, the stabbing and gushing blood, the dissection, and the final butchery. Farad, the only surviving witness, said that Jameson later displayed his works to the chiefs for their approval. The actual pictures were never produced as evidence and never surfaced.

If Ethel Jameson thought her husband's own account would persuade the public that he had been nothing but an innocent bystander, she was wrong.

A number of newspapers pointed out that Jameson was, by the time of the incident, no wide-eyed innocent. He had travelled with Tippu Tib, seen the slavers kill with impunity and even seen white officers kick and beat young slave boys to death. He must have known what would happen if he had teased the slave trader about the 'lies and travellers' tales'. On 23 March 1891, after the publication of the Jameson diaries, the *New York Times* noted:

'If Mr Jameson really thought the proposed act was "all a joke", credit is scarcely done to his intelligence.'

'He had at that time been more than a year in the country and ought to have understood native views of human life rather better than this implies. The facts against him, if not so bad as first made to appear, are, at least, distressing enough.'

The newspaper expressed sympathy for Mrs Jameson's efforts to save her husband's reputation, but concluded, 'It does not strike us that this hope can be realised in any large degree.' A British gentleman had sat and watched as young girl was butchered and eaten. He had even got out his sketch book and made careful drawings of the grisly scene. It was grotesque. Even those who had backed the Jameson family in their campaign to clear Sligo's name now largely deserted them.

There were whispers, never based on the facts that emerged, that Jameson had gone further and even partaken in the rite of cannibalism itself. Two years after the final, inglorious end of the Emin Pasha Relief Expedition, the good name of James Sligo Jameson had been forever tainted.

Emin Pasha himself, who had never wanted to leave the Congo with Stanley, had been deposed by his own, mutinous men who took advantage of confusion shown by the sudden appearance of a 'rescue mission'. After refusing to join Stanley's lap of honour around the world, Pasha joined the German East African company as an explorer and was killed by two Arab slave traders during a row at a remote station in the Congo Free State in October 1892.

Dr Thomas Heazle Parke, the expedition medic and saviour of Stanley, was the first Irishman to cross the continent of Africa. He had also been part of the mission to rescue Gordon at Khartoum. He died in Scotland in 1893 at the age of thirty-six, weakened by his terrible trials in the Congo. His body was returned to be buried in Drumsna, Co. Leitrim. A statue of him still stands outside the Natural History Museum on Merrion Street in Dublin.

Henry Morton Stanley returned to Britain, married and became a Liberal MP , he was given a knighthood in 1899 for services to the British Empire and died in London on 10 May 1904, having travelled a long and often dark road from the workhouse of his youth.

ANTOINE WALSH
THE IRISH SLAVERS OF EAST AFRICA AND
THE CARIBBEAN

The Irish hold a unique place in the history of the trans-Atlantic slave trade, white Europeans who were both slaves and slavers, depending on which way the political and economic winds were blowing from the seventeenth century onward. Irish people were transported to the West Indies as indentured labour after the Cromwellian conquest or profited enthusiastically from the triangular trade between Europe, Africa and the sugar islands, cast as victims or villains as circumstances changed. Irish soldiers of fortune sailed as privateers for the French crown, with licence to plunder enemy shipping, stores and ports at will, and when the opportunity arose, Irish merchants, seamen and financiers were amongst the most enthusiastic slave traders of the eighteenth century.

Oliver Cromwell sent the Irish to 'Hell or Barbados', formalising a practice that had begun earlier in the seventeenth century that saw many thousands of poor and defeated Catholic Irish sent to the Caribbean as virtual slaves to work on the plantations of North and South America, Montserrat, Antigua, Barbados and beyond; on the island of Barbados, final destination for up to twelve thousand Irish indentured servants (a conservative estimate, the British plantation owners they were sold to did not keep exact records) their descendants, the 'Redlegs' or 'poor whites' can still be found today.

However, while Cromwell offered transportation in chains, the restored Charles Stuart and his fellow European monarchs offered the Irish the chance to take the same journey in more comfortable quarters, or buy and sell countless thousands of Africans to do the job instead. Slaving was not only hugely profitable, it was also respectable, with the Europeans involved conveniently classifying slaves sold to them by local rulers as prisoners of war who would face a quick death at the hands of their native enemies unless they were offered new and exciting employment opportunities on Christian-run plantations across the Atlantic.

The many Haitians and West Indians who trace their ancestry back to African slaves transported on Irish-owned slave ships are living proof that the Irish have not always been the victims of history. The vast profits would establish Irish slaving dynasties, with the Irish of Nantes in France – closely-affiliated clans of sailors and slavers – making the kind of money that allowed some to eventually join the French nobility.

When Charles II returned to the throne in 1660, the West Indies were already becoming the motor of global trade, with white gold from the sugar cane plantations making huge fortunes in Europe. The entrepreneurial Irish got in on the ground floor with figures like William Ronan, an Irish Catholic and officer of the Royal Africa Company, engaging directly in the trade of humans on the Slave Coast of East Africa in the late seventeenth century. Ronan rose to become the chairman of the Chief Merchants of the Royal African Company at Cape Castle in modern day Ghana, effectively running one of the world's biggest slave trading ports during a decade in Africa (1687-1697). His work must have impressed his royal and commercial shareholders at home as he continued in his job after the rise of the Protestant William of Orange to the thrones of England, Scotland and Ireland.

The ascent of William of Orange also created an opportunity for another Irishman, a Dublin-born merchant (whose family originally hailed from Kilkenny) who would go on to found one of the great Irish piracy and slaving dynasties.

Philip Walsh was the son of James Walsh, of Ballynacooly in the Walsh Mountains in Co. Kilkenny and at one time a captain in the Royal French navy. He was present at the signing of the Treaty of Limerick on 3 October 1691, which marked the end of the Williamite War in Ireland between the Jacobites and the supporters of William of Orange. The treaty allowed Jacobite soldiers who had fought for the Catholic King James II to leave the country, either going with James to France to fight in the Irish Brigade – *La Brigade Irlandaise* – or seeking service in the French, Spanish or Austrian armies. In the chaos that followed the end of the war, thousands of exiled Irish soldiers and commanders would be blown across the sea to the continent or west to North America.

Some fourteen thousand Jacobite soldiers, together with their families, chose to march south to Cork to embark for France, part of what became known as the Flight of the Wild Geese; they would serve the French King and the fading dream of a Stuart restoration for a hundred years until the French revolution. Many would die serving in foreign armies; a few shrewd ones would establish new businesses, properties and dynasties abroad, making fortunes in everything from wine to slavery.

James Walsh, together with his son, Philip, commanded the ship that carried the defeated King James II from Kinsale in Co. Cork to France after the battle of the Boyne. In fact, over the years, the family were a sort of personal taxi service for the Stuarts during their ill-fated adventures, Philip's son Antoine Vincent was the owner/operator of the armed frigate *Doutelle*, the ship that landed Charles Stuart, James II's son and the 'Young Pretender', in Scotland in 1745. The *Doutelle* and a sister ship, the *Elisabeth*, left the port of Belleisle on 5 July 1745 to bring Charles to the waiting Scottish clans who would support his bid for the throne.

The ships ran into trouble on 9 July when they were spotted by a British man-o-war, the sixty-gun *Lion*, west of the Lizard at the tip of Cornwall and the *Elisabeth* was engaged in a ferocious battle. After five hours of broadside-to-broadside fighting, both ships were severely damaged and it was said that Prince Charles urged Antoine Walsh to go to the aid of the stricken *Elisabeth*. Walsh, a fearless, determined and ruthless captain, refused point blank to go to the French ship's aid and warned the prince that if he didn't pipe down, he would have him escorted below to his cabin. Bonnie Prince Charlie had a brief enough stay in Scotland, but Antoine was knighted for going along on the enterprise, becoming the first Earl Walsh.

That the Young Pretender and the Irish adventurer and slaver enjoyed a very close relationship was revealed when a remarkable cache of documents from the era was discovered at the Walsh ancestral Chateau in France in 1901. Historians were puzzled by a series of letters, addressed to a 'M. Le Grand', and signed 'Douglas' or 'J. Douglas'. The mysterious air of the letters, and their friendly tone, though the sentiments clearly came from someone of great importance, intrigued the editors of the documents until another letter was discovered, addressed by Prince Charles Stuart to 'M. Antoine Walsh', which solved the riddle; Bonnie Prince Charlie had devised code-names for himself and Antoine Walsh, as his majesty himself explained in the letter to his Irish friend and supporter. 'Henceforth,' wrote the Prince to Walsh, 'you will address me as M. Douglas, and bear in mind that you are always and for everybody to be M. Legrand.'

Antoine's father, Philip, had settled in St Malo in Brittany (where Anthony or Antoine was born on 22 January 1703) and looked at start-up opportunities in the burgeoning Atlantic slave trade. Philip Walsh was a shipbuilder, merchant and at times a daring and ruthless privateer or licensed pirate for the French crown, with free rein to attack and capture British shipping in the English Channel when the two great European powers were at war. He sailed fast, heavily-armed, but relatively small ships such as *Le Curieux* under letters of marque from the French crown.

These letters of marque were a wartime expedient that allowed warring nations to sub-contract the work of war at sea out to private ship owners. These privateers would be licensed to attack and seize enemy vessels and property, which would then be brought before a court that decided how the spoils were shared out. The lion's share of the 'prize' went to the captain (thus ensuring enthusiastic efforts at sea against the enemy) with the crown also getting a healthy share. It was licensed piracy, patriotism for profit, with the many risks (such as running into a more heavily-armed enemy force) more than compensated for by the huge bounties to be won. The French used the term '*lettre de course*' for their letters of marque, giving rise to the term 'corsair'.

The main target would have been enemy merchant men within close range as privateers often skimped on provisions to increase speed. But Philip Walsh would venture far in search of a prize, on one occasion taking two ships, the *Ruby* and *Diligent,* into the Indian Ocean and on another, sailing *Le Curieux* around Africa and to the mouth of the Red Sea to attack Dutch-owned coffee stores in Moka in the Yemen. On that raid against the largest coffee market on the coast of Arabia, the Irish corsair captain plundered an estimated 1,500 tonnes of the highest-quality coffee beans. Philip, who married an Irish woman called Anne White and had ten children, died on a later voyage to Africa.

It was left to one of his sons, Antoine, to get the real family business – slaving – off the ground. In fact, it was the huge wealth that he generated through the slave trade that allowed him to get into the Pretender-transporting trade when Bonnie Price Charlie came looking for a lift to Scotland. Walsh and his fellow Irish merchants even covered the transportation costs, contributing the then sizable sum of £3,800.

By the early 1700s, the French port of Nantes, with a large, close-knit and hard-working Irish slave-trading community, became the chief slaving port for the kingdom of Louis XIV, the Sun King. It was said that half of the ships that sailed out of Nantes at the time were owned or stocked by Irish merchant families, including the Joyces, Walshes, MacCarthys, O'Sheils, Sarsfields and O'Riordans. Manufactured goods, guns, textiles, liquor and knives, were brought from Nantes to the Slave Coast, exchanged for slaves who were transported to the French colonies of Guadeloupe, Martinique and Saint-Domingue (modern Haiti) where they were sold for sugar and tobacco, which then returned to Europe. The Irish merchants built fine homes on the Île Feydeau, which still stand today, but the profits were spread far beyond Nantes: they made fortunes for the ports of Bristol, Liverpool and Amsterdam. To their great credit, the merchants of Belfast, under the future United Irishman William Putnam McCabe, refused to take part in the inhuman slave trade. However, the merchant princes of Cork, Limerick and Waterford profited by victualling the ships, feeding the slavers and slaves alike to great reward and family fortune. Huge family fortunes were built in Cork, and the city centre was rebuilt; some of those dynasties that were built on the backs and bellies of millions of slaves are still with us today. And so it went on for decades, with the wealth of nations and Empires built up on unimaginable human misery.

The history of the French slave trade was long, barbarous and massively-profitable for almost everybody involved, from the Arab slavers and local rulers in West Africa who supplied to the human cargoes to the slavers who transported them across the Atlantic, the plantation owners who put them to work and the financiers and pillars of society who provided the capital and collected the profits. It is estimated that in the history of the Atlantic slave trade, the French enslaved four times as many Africans as the Americans; research carried out by the eminent African-American historian and activist W.E.B Dubois (amongst others) estimates that during the course of legal slave trading carried out by France, some 4,200 slave voyages were made, transporting a total of one-and-a-quarter million Africans to French territories. This compares to around 1,500 slaver voyages made to British North America/United States with a total of approximately three hundred thousand slaves. The French not only started trading in slaves earlier than the Americans or British, they continued to countenance the trade until 1830, long after the rest of Europe had outlawed it; 'illegal' trading (mostly carried out by Cuban-based slavers working for French interests) continued until at least the end of the American Civil War in 1865.

Conditions on French possessions such as the island of Haiti were more barbarous and brutal than those in the southern states of the United States of America. As a result, the French needed far more slaves than the Americans because of the relatively short life-expectancy of those forced to work on their plantations (in reality, massive and intensive agri-factories). Once a slave started work in the sugar fields, putting in shifts of sixteen to nineteen hours a day during the growing and harvesting season (November to May) their average life expectancy shrank to eight years. Brutality was rife. Slaves were regularly whipped to death for minor transgressions or hideously injured and killed in accidents in the fields or in the processing plants. Slave revolts were common and the plantation owners and authorities used almost unimaginable brutality to hold their massive slave populations down.

In French-controlled North America, conditions could be just as bad. When the US acquired Louisiana from France in 1803, the first governor sent out from Washington reported back: 'No subject seems to be so interesting to the minds of the inhabitants of all parts of the country which I have visited as that of the importation of brute negroes from Africa. This permission would go further with them, and better reconcile them to the government of the United States, than any other privilege that could be extended to this country ... White labourers, they say, cannot be had in this unhealthy climate.'

On Saint Domingue, modern day Haiti, the French West Indian Company established its colony/corporation in 1664. By the second half of the eighteenth century, Saint Domingue was a massively-profitable operation for its French investors and (occasionally Irish) plantation owners and one of the richest colonies in the French empire. By the late 1780s, Saint-Domingue was producing around 40 per cent of all the sugar and 60 per cent of all the coffee consumed in Europe. A single colony, roughly the size of Belgium and with a slave population estimated at 460,000 Africans, was producing more sugar and coffee that all of Britain's West Indian territories combined. In one year in the late 1780s, well over six hundred vessels visited the ports of Saint Domingue, delivering fresh slaves for the fields and carrying off sugar, coffee, cotton, indigo and cacao to a hungry European market.

The brutal conditions and high turn-over in slave labour meant that Saint-Domingue needed a constant re-supply of human beasts of burden from Africa, as many as forty thousand per year by the late 1780s. And a small but dedicated band of Irish slavers, running thriving family concerns out of the Atlantic ports of northern France, were hard at work dealing with the demand.

Antoine Walsh was, until he was comfortable enough to retire to an office job on land, a slave ship captain. The voyage, from France to East Africa and then across the Atlantic to the Caribbean, was long and perilous and those making it faced everything from disease and foul weather to the possibility of piracy and mutinous human cargoes.

By the early 1730s, Walsh had seen enough of the disease-ridden coast of East Africa and the dangers of the middle passage and promoted himself from slave-ship captain to slave-merchant.

Antoine had been lucky enough to avoid the bloody below-decks uprisings that claimed the lives of many slavers, including some of his employees and relatives. In 1734, the slave ship

L'Aventurier, outfitted by Walsh's father-in-law Luc O'Shiel (a former Jacobite officer), spent nearly four months moving up and down the West African coast, looking for slaves.

At Ouida (also called 'Whydah' by the slavers) on the coast of Benin, the captain (a J. Shaughnessy) went ashore to trade, leaving Barnaby O'Shiel, Antoine's young brother-in-law, in command of a crew laid low by fever and dysentery. The slaves took their chance and broke free, cutting the barely-conscious pilot's throat and locking the other invalid sailors below hatches. It was up to young Barnaby to rally the five sailors who could carry a gun; in the ensuing fight to regain the ship two crewmen and forty slaves were killed. In commercial terms, they had lost one-sixth of the cargo and Captain Shaughnessy was forced to tie up at Ouida until he had collected 480 men, women and children to transport in chains to Saint-Domingue and Martinique. Both Barnaby and Shaughnessy survived to have careers as slaver captains for Antoine.

There were other ship revolts, including a bloody escape attempt on Antoine's ironically-named *Prince d'Orange* that began after six women, one carrying a child, threw themselves overboard and drowned just as the ship was making sail. The *Prince d'Orange* did sail with almost 250 slaves on board, but after one month at sea, off the island of San Thome, the remaining slaves rose and killed the captain and two sailors. The crew did eventually restore order, but not before thirty-six Africans lay dead on the bloody deck. An officer named John Hanratty took over as captain and delivered the cargo.

In almost a half-century of operations by Irish slave ships sailing out of the Breton ports, there was only one successful slave rising. In 1742, the 350 slaves aboard merchant Patrick Archer's *La Sainte Hélène* managed to seize the ship's firearms, set the vessel on fire and escape to the shore, where they were given sanctuary by a local ruler.

Antoine Walsh would suffer a major setback after 1748 when he attempted to monopolise the French-East African slave trade by setting up the ambitious Societé d'Angole, the first private joint stock company in France devoted to the slave trade. The company was to have three large trade ships permanently stationed off the East African coast with five smaller ships to transport their cargoes to fortified slave camps in modern day Haiti. Walsh could not defeat his rivals and was forced out of the slave trade, leaving France to manage the family slave plantations in Sainte Domingue (Haiti) where he died in 1763.

Ten years earlier, in 1753, Antoine had been enobled by King Louis XV of France and the family estates on the lower Loire were consolidated by Royal letters-patent into the 'Comte de Serrant'. The Walshes were henceforth Comtes de Serrant.

The exiled Irishman had personally bought and sold over twelve thousand African slaves and launched forty cross-Atlantic slave voyages. He was the greatest – or worst – of the Irish-Nantes slavers, far outstripping rivals such as the O'Riordan brothers, Etienne and Laurent, who had family back in Derryvoe, Co. Cork. The Roches, originally from Limerick, where their extended clan included Arthurs and Suttons, managed a mere eleven slave voyages with around three thousand slaves. At the height of the trade, Irish and French merchants in Nantes kept so many African men and women in their fine houses that they could give *négrillons* or *négrittes* (child slaves) to members of their household as tips. By the time of the French Revolution there were enough *nègres* in Nantes to form a battalion – which earned a dreadful reputation for murder and pillage.

As the slave trade declined in France and moved to Liverpool and Bristol towards the end of the eighteenth century, other Irish families, the Callaghans and Teagues of Bristol and David Tuohy, a Tralee-born, Liverpool merchant, would continue the long Irish tradition in the purchase and sale of Africans. An estimated one in ten of the sailors manning the British slavers were Irish and some of them – including John Carren, John Megan and James Gallagher – sailed under an English captain called John Newton during the 1750s. Newton, who transported thousands of slaves in abject misery, would later repent of his sins, become an Anglican clergyman and write the great hymn of redemption, 'Amazing Grace'. The hymn was written after Newton, during a terrible storm, called on the Lord to save him and his ship. He continued to work in the slave trade for some years after it was written, though he became known for insisting that his human cargoes be treated humanely. Newton, who educated himself and became an evangelical preacher and churchman, did later repent fully of his sins in human bondage, directly inspiring the great anti-slavery campaigner William Wilberforce. 'Amazing Grace' became to the campaigners against slavery what 'We Shall Overcome' was to the civil-rights activists of the twentieth century.

Newton's memorial is the hymn; Antoine Walsh left us the magnificent Renaissance Chateau de Serrant between Angers and Nantes, which he bought and renovated in 1749. The Chateau passed out of the Walsh family's direct ownership in 1830 when Antoine's descendant Valentine Walsh de Serrant married the Duc de La Trémoille. The castle remains in the Trémoille family and the monumental gate erected by Antoine still stands today, bearing the Walsh family arms. Those arms feature a swan pierced by an arrow and the motto '*Transfixus sed non mortuus*' or 'Pierced but not dead'.

Balzac's observation, 'Behind every great fortune there is a great crime', might be more apt.

LUKE RYAN

BENJAMIN FRANKLIN'S IRISH PIRATE

L uke Ryan may not have been the most famous pirate to ever command a ship, but in a profession that demanded quick wits, reckless bravery and the ability to talk your way out of a tight corner, the charismatic Dublin man could certainly have claimed to be among the craftiest.

The mid to late eighteenth century was an extraordinary time in Irish, European and American history, when Irish sailors and captains put to sea in heavily-armed, privately-owned and licensed pirate ships, fighting for and against the Yankees, British and French. Some made fortunes; some were strung up or lost in battle or shipwreck. Only one would be remembered as a hero of the American Revolution, even if it was never exactly clear just who Luke Ryan was fighting for; Ryan's fleet, which included the infamous *Black Prince*, was part of a private navy (that included three Irish captains and hundreds of Irish sailors) commissioned by Benjamin Franklin to take the war to the British in their home waters.

At a time when the fledgling United States was fighting for its very existence, facing the might of the British Empire, Luke Ryan and many Irishmen like him fought the Royal Navy and targeted vital mercantile interests in Britain's home waters, offering hope to the hard-pressed Americans and giving King George, his ministers and admirals pause for thought.

Dublin, and especially the smaller ports around it, was a hotbed of smuggling and semi-legal piracy in the period of the American Revolutionary War, offering plenty of chances for men who were willing to take a risk. Dubliner Luke Ryan was one of hundreds of young Irishmen who seized the chance to make their fortunes in uncertain times as Britain, France and the United States went to war.

By the time he reached his mid-twenties, Ryan was the most notorious and most successful privateer captain operating in British waters, even if the British, whom he fought, and the Americans, whom he served, had little idea of his true identity. Like all the best pirates, he was devious, avoiding the Royal Navy's men-o-war where possible, hiding his true role as captain behind stooges and changing flags, nationalities and his very identity as the situation demanded. However, he would use any tactics he deemed necessary, from fire and murder to jailbreaks, kidnapping, ransom and extortion, to add to his fortune. All ships were fair game to the spectacularly-successful young captain born in Rush, Co. Dublin.

And when he was finally captured at sea as a self-declared French officer, serving both King Louis XVI and the United States of America, he claimed French and then American citizenship before being tried and condemned to death at the Old Bailey as an Irish subject of the British Crown.

Found guilty of High Treason and the Piratical Taking of Ships at Sea (or 'mayhem, murder and mutiny' as the Admiralty Court heard), Luke Ryan would survive four appointments with the hangman, only to lose his considerable fortune to unscrupulous French bankers and then lose his life in a Debtors' Prison. When he died, the influential *Gentleman's Magazine* of London noted that Ryan's command had 'captured more vessels belonging to Great Britain than any other single ship during the war. The various scenes he went through are astonishing.'

Benjamin Franklin's links to pirates and privateers began in December 1776, when, newly-arrived in France as ambassador for the fledgling United States of America – then thirteen states, former colonies of the British that had declared their independence – he was facing what appeared to be an intractable problem. North America still had significant numbers of people who were loyal to the British crown, but from New Hampshire down the east coast to Georgia, the newly-declared states had struck for what seemed to be an impossible goal, independence from the vastly-powerful British Empire. The Americans would find willing allies in Britain's great rival France. But in 1776, they were in a desperate, almost hopeless position as they took on what was then the globe's pre-eminent military and economic power. And while the Revolutionary War raged in Continental America, across the Atlantic in England hundreds of American citizens, mostly seamen seized in British ports on on the high seas, were being held in prisons with no recourse to winning their freedom.

Franklin was deeply concerned with the plight of his fellow Americans and arranged for money and supplies to be provided for the men held in two prisons, The Old Mill Prison in Plymouth and Forton Prison in Portsmouth. Some prisoners had been able to escape. Franklin, a brilliant spy-master as well as scientist and statesman, was able to set up networks that would smuggle these Americans to the friendlier shores of France.

Under the normal rules of war at the time belligerent states could arrange for the swapping of prisoners and there were regular exchanges of captured soldiers and sailors between France and Britain. However, as the American revolutionaries were seen as merely rebellious British subjects, they were not entitled to be returned to America. If captured by the British, either on land or at sea, they would be held in one of His Majesty's Prisons, treated as rebels and denied any chance of freedom, exchange or parole. To make matters more galling for Franklin and the Americans, any British prisoners captured by American forces and taken to French territory would have to be returned as part of the regular system of exchange between the British and French.

Franklin solved his legal problem by signing the Treaty of Alliance with France on 6 February 1778. This treaty made France and the United States allies in the fight against the British and allowed the Americans, now involved in raiding British sea commerce, to hold British prisoners in French ports. Franklin had won recognition for the United States from the French and effectively forced the British to agree to exchange combatants. All he needed now were some human bargaining chips. And that was where men like Luke Ryan would come in.

Luke Ryan was born outside the Co. Dublin village of Rush on 14 February 1750, the only son of Michael and Mary Ryan of the parish of Kenure. As a young man, he had worked on the fishing and trading boats that sailed out of Rush and also worked for the local estate as a stable-hand from the age of ten. At twelve he started work in a boatyard and was then apprenticed to Edward King of Ringsend as a ship's carpenter in 1766. Luke appears to have been a restless youth and after giving up his apprenticeship, he found his way to Dunkirk in France to join Dillon's Regiment, one of the regiments making up the Irish Brigade of 'Wild Geese' (Irish soldiers who left for the continent after the Williamite wars of the previous century) fighting in the service of the French crown.

The Wild Geese had been scattered across the continent and the tradition of Irishmen fighting under foreign flags, for the French, Spanish, Austrians, and various Italian states, would continue right up to the twentieth-century. This tradition would also see Irishmen fight and die on both sides of the American Civil War, on a number of occasions coming into direct conflict on the battlefield, such as during the terrible slaughter at Gettysburg and at Fredericksburg in December 1862.

Ryan might have remained as one of the thousands of Irishmen fighting on the continent if it was not for the outbreak of the American War of Independence. When war started in 1775, the Americans could just about prevent their citizen militias from being overrun and decimated by British forces in the thirteen former colonies. On land, the nascent Continental Army was fighting for its survival against significantly more powerful and experienced British forces. Conventional war at sea against the vast power of the Royal Navy was inconceivable.

But hit-and-run tactics were just about workable for small, fast, heavily-armed and expertly-sailed US ships. And if these 'experts' couldn't be found within the ranks of the US navy proper, then the Americans could use the ancient practice of outfitting and licensing private warships or 'privateers', simply by issuing them with 'letters of marque' – government licences allowing the holder to attack vessels owned by the enemy and bring them before the admiralty. Privateers could also claim the right to act against port installations or even civilian property and goods on enemy land, under the cry of 'seize, burn or destroy'. It was often desperate, cut-throat work, involving long sea chases, brief but bloody engagements, lightning raids, kidnapping-for-ransom and trickery (privateers would carry many flags and use any and all deception to lure in unsuspecting victims).

Though 'privateers' with a letter of marque worked for profit, it could be considered a patriotic occupation and was certainly considered to be several steps above out-and-out piracy. However, they occupied a hazy legal ground, half-way between pirates and ships of national navies, and some, like Ryan, were not against acting as smugglers and out-and-out pirates.

By the second year of the War of Independence, the American Continental Navy was already beginning to cause havoc in the channel and the Irish Sea. Commissioned officers such as the legendary Scottish-born captain John Paul Jones (in the *Ranger*) and the Maryland merchant captain turned US navy commander Lambert Wickes, launched daring raids along the coast of Scotland, England, Wales and Ireland.

Early in 1777, the Dublin newspapers were carrying alarming reports of three US privateers, the *Lexington*, *Reprisal* and *Dolphin*, sweeping down the Irish Sea and seizing thirteen British vessels, which were either burnt or taken under sail to France. At the same time, there were reports that smugglers in Rush, north county Dublin (home port of Luke Ryan) had attacked and driven off Revenue men and militia sent to stop their illegal trade. The newspapers carried warnings of the great threat to vital Irish Sea merchant trade (including the highly-valuable linen ships that sailed from Ireland) with reports that crafty Irish smugglers were hoisting American colours, in order to 'avoid the interruption the revenue cutters might give to their trade'.

Amidst the growing lawlessness, public outcry and dire warnings that Yankee pirates were coming to cut the throats of Dublin merchants while they slept in their beds, the British government came under increasing pressure to act. The Royal Navy, already struggling to supply the forces fighting in the US, began to recruit privateers in Ireland and Britain to meet fire with fire. At the start of 1778, a smuggler turned privateer, captained by John Harding of Loughshinny in Fingal, north county Dublin, was ready to sail from Dublin with a crew of around 150 local men. Their ship was called, fittingly enough, the *Dublin*. The Fingallian sailors were renowned as some of the toughest and most skilled sailors in Europe, seasoned by long and arduous fishing voyages and ready to turn smuggler and outfox the Revenue men whenever the chance arose. Fast and heavily-armed, the ship had a letter of marque from the English and sailed as an Irish privateer against the Yankees.

Luke Ryan, who had become a partner in a lucrative smuggling operation with a cousin of his called Edward Wilde out of Loughshinny, was soon getting in on the act, converting their smuggling vessel, the *Friendship* to go to war. In February 1778, the *Friendship* finished outfitting at Sir John Rogerson's Quay in Dublin and put to sea as a privateer. She was a fast cutter, armed with six eighteen-pounder guns, able to chase down and then close with her prey, which, as she was sailing under a letter of marque from the English crown, was supposed to be American shipping.

However, Ryan, the former French soldier who had connections to the privateer's port of Dunkirk in France, must have decided that as Yankee ships were hard to come by (and devilishly hard to take) there were far richer pickings in the British merchantmen who crowded into the channel, bringing treasure and trade from all over the world to the ports of southern England.

Ryan may have set out with a British letter of marque, but in early 1779, the *Friendship* had a secret change of ownership, with Ryan and his partner Wilde (who sometimes went by the *nom-de-guerre* 'McCatter') entering the service of the Dunkirk-based businessman Jean Francois Torris. The Irish-owned ship had effectively changed sides and was now acting for French backers against the British, with the American revolutionaries set to benefit from their activities.

Jean Francois Torris was an *armateur* – a middleman who supplied the capital needed to arm, outfit and commission the privateers – and his native Dunkirk was a privateer's port, as close to a pirate town as you could get in northern Europe in the latter half of the eighteenth century. Privateering in Dunkirk was big business and was administrated by the French civil service; revenue came from charging rewards, fines and duties levied on behalf of Louis XVI. The French government supplied the port facilities for the conversion and fitting out of smuggling vessels and sold former naval ships for privateering. The town was a magnet for rogues and adventurers of all nations, drawn by the prospects of high-rewards for high-risks. And now, through his controlling stake in the *Friendship*, the Frenchman Torris was in the slightly strange position of owning a privateer crewed and commanded by Irishmen and (nominally, at least) carrying a letter of marque from the English admiralty.

The Irish smuggling ship, turned British letter of marque was now a renegade French privateer. And it was bound for Dublin in May 1779 with a cargo of brandy and other contraband goods, to turn a profit for its French owner. However, the ship ran foul of the ever-vigilant Revenue men, who seized the *Friendship* and its crew at Rogerstown near Rush shortly after they docked.

Wilde and his crew were thrown into the Black Dog Prison, close to the quays in the heart of Dublin at Cornmarket. Ryan, by now a very worldly twenty-five-year-old, had not been on board when the ship and its crew was seized and soon hit on a plan to free his crew and retake the *Friendship*. He organised a force of smugglers from Rush to go up the River Liffey in armed river ferry boats, they subdued the guards in the dead of night and sprung Wilde and the rest of the men from the Black Dog. They then boarded the *Friendship*, cut the anchor lines and sailed her back to Rush, along with a small group of unwilling passengers, Revenue men who had been surprised on board the ship by the sudden arrival of the men from Rush. After taking on additional crew in an inlet in north county Dublin, Ryan sportingly dropped the Dublin Revenue officers across the Irish Sea in Dorset before making away for Dunkirk.

Once out of reach of the British Revenue and navy at Dunkirk, it was time for Luke Ryan and the *Friendship* to change their identities and sign up to help Benjamin Franklin win the War of Independence.

Franklin had been on the lookout for likely vessels to carry American letters of marque. Jean François Torris was able to offer the American ambassador to the court of King Louis XVI some likely candidates, and top of the list was the lightning-fast Irish cutter with its enterprising captain and a crew that, after the Black Dog breakout, owed Ryan their lives and their liberty. Torris sold Franklin on the idea – the *Friendship* would be renamed the *Black*

Prince and her Irish crew would sail under American colours.

Torris and Ryan wanted profit. Franklin wanted chaos. It was a mutually-beneficial arrangement even if there was one slight sticking point; as a pirate wanted by the British, Luke Ryan could not legally command a US privateer. So Torris and the Dubliner came up with a simple solution, an unemployed merchant seaman from Boston called Stephen Marchant would be the nominal captain and front-man for the operation. Ben Franklin was told the *Black Prince* was sailing under an American captain. But it was a twenty-five-year-old Dubliner – a pirate, smuggler and wanted man – who was really calling the shots.

The *Black Prince* went to work, sailing from Dunkirk in June 1779 and quickly snapping up eight British prizes which were sailed back to the French port of Morlaix. In July, Ryan and his ship captured a further thirteen British coastal trading vessels, which were stripped of their cargoes and then ransomed back to the English owners. A Waterford brig (a quick and highly-manoeuvrable ship with two square-rigged masts) called the *Sally-Anne* was one of eighteen vessels brought into the ports of Morlaix and Dunkirk after a particularly productive cruise to the waters off the south west coast of England. In September, the *Black Prince*, which now included another Rush man as officer, one Patrick Dowling, went on a longer cruise, all the way up to the Outer Hebrides off the far north west coast of Scotland to seize an impressive thirty-four prizes.

Part of the secret of the *Black Prince's* success was its ability to stalk its prey while projecting a pacific appearance. Sailing with its gun-ports closed (but with slow-match burning and cannon-fully loaded, ready to be run out at a moment's command) it could look like an innocent trading vessel. Privateers like Ryan would go to such lengths as making their ships look scruffy, ill-handled and as different from a tautly-sailed and obviously disciplined and dangerous man-o-war as possible. It was only when you got up close to the cutter that you might notice the extra gun-ports, the seventy-odd, evil-looking crewmen packed on deck and the murderous swivel guns bolted to the rails.

By then it was usually too late. Ryan and his crew were close enough and well-armed enough to threaten a broadside that would blow your ship to matchsticks. If you resisted and they were able to board with cutlasses, flintlock pistols and deadly musketoons (a primitive form of shot-gun, often loaded with glass or old nails) they would make short and bloody work of any resistance. Worthy prizes were sailed back to friendly ports to be stripped, sold or ransomed back to their owners. Vessels that didn't warrant that effort were burned to the waterline. Ryan, the smuggler, contraband runner and sometimes fisherman, knew the waters around Britain and Ireland like few others.

Benjamin Franklin was impressed. There was consternation in London, where the *Black Prince* was now causing great dread and distress to the merchants and money men of the City. By this stage, the nominal American captain Marchant had given up his paper command and returned to the US, to leave the Irish to get on with the job. Torris and Matthew Wilde (or 'McCatter') sourced a new vessel, which was named the privateer *Black Princess* and put to sea. Their trusted Rush compatriot, Patrick Dowling, would take over the *Black Prince* under an American commission.

Ryan, who had been ill, now wanted to come out of the shadows. Together with Torris, he wrote to Benjamin Franklin seeking permission to outfit a new privateer with the Rush man as captain, sailing, officially for the first time, with an American commission. Franklin was now in on the secret. He realised that he had been hoodwinked by Torris and Ryan. But the Founding Father was impressed. He recognised in Ryan the kind of successful leader of men who could get the job done. And it was war, whatever the legal niceties. He responded by buying a new ship, the former French man-o-war *Sans Peur* (or the *Fear Not* to her English-speaking crew), making Ryan its official master (though not making him an official commissioned officer of the American navy) and setting her on British shipping. Franklin also presented Ryan with a highly-prized 'night glass', a telescope that had been specially adapted to make the most of dim light. Franklin may have been exercising his noted sense of humour as a night glass was the perfect accessory for a pirate.

The *Fear Not* was refitted and sailed in early 1780 for the Orkney Islands, where she seized sixteen prizes on her first voyage under her new master, Luke Ryan. With eighteen cannon and twelve swivel guns, the *Fear Not* was a match for many armed ships and could claim to justify her defiant name.

There were now three Irish-commanded and crewed ships sailing under American commission for Benjamin Franklin against the British. And while Wilde and Dowling were doing their bit for the Revolution, it was Ryan in the *Fear Not* who was really making a name for himself. The ship caused mayhem along the Scottish coast. When supplies ran low, *Fear Not* sailed into one of the more isolated ports and demanded victualling at the point of eighteen cannon. On more than one occasion, Ryan was said to have blown up the storehouses of a Scots merchant who was not coming across with the goods.

On 28 July 1780, the Dublin newspaper, *The Freeman's Journal*, reported on 'letters recently arrived from Scotland', which 'mentioned that the *Fearnought* [sic] privateer, Luke Ryan commander, landed at Stornaway, in the island of Lewis, and after plundering the town, carried off the principal inhabitants hostages, as ransomers for the houses.' To the British, Ryan and his men were fighting for the Americans, but they were not American citizens, they were Irish pirates and rebels. If captured, it was the hangman's noose in short order. But as one American officer who came into contact with Ryan observed, 'I have sailed with many brave men, but none the equal to this Captain Luke Ryan for skill and bravery.'

Torris, the hard-nosed French armateur, also appears to have had a soft spot for Ryan. On at least one occasion he is said to have asked Benjamin Franklin to accede to Ryan's request for a formal commission in the Continental Navy and US citizenship. Ryan himself wrote that he would give 'the last drop of blood to gain honour for the American flag.' Franklin never did make Ryan and his men an official part of the Continental Navy, with the protections that this would have brought. They always operated in the para-legal world of the privateer. The American ambassador to the French court may simply have not had time to formalise Ryan's status further; but it is also possible that when it came to dealing with the British, as it surely must, it suited Franklin and his fellow politicians to have plausible deniability of the Irish privateers. Negotiations with the defeated British would be difficult enough without having to admit to employing Irish rebels and pirates who sailed under all flags and none, in shadowy waters between the law and lawlessness.

Franklin may also have been irked by Ryan and his fellow captains' failure to bring in as many prisoners as he wanted for exchange. Strangely, the Irish privateers seemed to be more intent on treasure than the more complicated business of catching and holding British prisoners.

As the *Fear Not* joined the *Black Prince* and *Black Princess* at sea, the British navy came under increasing pressure to do something. There were reports in the English newspapers that two Royal Navy frigates had been sent out to look for the Irish privateers.

Luke Ryan and his fellow Irish privateers were about to become the victims of their own success. Since the middle of 1779, events had gone Ryan's way. He had sailed in and commanded five different privateers, *Black Prince, Black Princess, Fear Not, La Marechal* and *Calonne,* capturing an impressive 114 prizes. He had ransomed seventy-five captains of British vessels and exchanged over 160 British seamen. He and his fellow privateers from Rush had sailed under three different flags (not counting flags of deception) and fought on both sides of the war, albeit briefly for the British. In a little over two years, they had been by far the most active and successful captains in a privateering fleet that had destroyed 733 British and Irish prizes with cargoes valued in excess of two million pounds.

During a debate in the British House of Lords at the end of the Revolutionary War in 1783, peers were told that the actions of Yankee privateers during the recent conflict had cost the British merchant navy an estimated £8m in damages. This did not take into account the huge problems caused to the British war effort and the Royal Navy, which was effectively forced to fight a sea war on the 'wrong' side of the Atlantic. Benjamin Franklin's proxy sea war, fought with American captains and Irish and French privateers, had worked even better than he could have hoped.

But by the summer of 1780, the mayhem being wrought at sea meant that the always murky issue of American letters of marque was a major diplomatic problem for the French, British and Americans. With all three nations coming to the realisation that the war would have to end, the French were becoming particularly irritated by actions of the privateers who were turning their waters into a lawless zone. The American Congress, not happy to have the wild Irish plundering international trade in their name, responded to growing pressure from the French and instructed a reluctant

Franklin to revoke the commissions given to non-Americans sailing (nominally) under the thirteen-striped flag of the US. As a congressman and ambassador, Franklin was bound by the views of his government. Those captains and sailors who were not American citizens were going to be cut loose to fend for themselves.

As the politicians manoeuvred in the background, it was business as usual for Ryan, who had by now taken command of the three-decked, thirty-two-gun frigate *Calonne,* purchased by Torris from the French navy and crewed by 250 men. Ryan had also secured French citizenship for himself, as a protection against summary execution as a rebellious Irish pirate. Or so he thought. He remained unaware that Benjamin Franklin and the American Congress would no longer offer American protection to 'foreign'-crewed letters of marque.

The end came for Luke Ryan off the Firth of Forth on the coast of Scotland in April 1781. In the waters off St Abbe's Head, Ryan's frigate *Calonne,* under French colours and crewed by 250 Irish, Dutch, French and American sailors, had captured a fat little prize, the merchant brig *Nancy.* Luke Ryan wanted to deal with business quickly and bargained a ransom with the *Nancy's* master, a Captain John Ramsay. A price of three hundred guineas was agreed and the *Nancy* was cut loose. Captain Ramsay would stay on board the *Calonne* as a guest of Luke Ryan until the agreed ransom had been handed over. As dusk began to fall on the evening of 16 April, Ryan's lookout shouted 'sail-ho!' as a number of ships were spotted on the horizon. Ryan was suspicious, a force of ships spotted in enemy waters would certainly give him pause for thought. But Ramsey, a quick-thinking Scot, observed to his captor that the ships were bound to be Greenland whalers, on their way to the Arctic. Unarmed whalers meant rich pickings and Ryan fell for what turned out to be expertly-proffered bait.

The 'easy prizes' turned out to be nothing of the kind. The *Calonne* was actually running up to the *Berwick,* a Royal Navy first-rater of seventy-four guns. And worse, the *Berwick* had an escort, the two-decker, thirty-six-gun *Belle Poule,* which had manoeuvred in the failing light to come up behind the *Calonne* and was quickly opening up with broadsides. Ryan immediately engaged the *Belle Poule,* hoping that he could knock away a mast and make his escape before the *Berwick* could come up and catch him between two fires. But after a heavy exchange of guns, lasting an hour, the *Berwick* did arrive and Ryan was forced to strike his colours.

Ryan was initially treated as a French officer, until Captain Patton of the *Berwick* noticed that this French gentleman did not have a great command of his own language, and seemed to speak with what sounded suspiciously like a rough Irish accent. The *Calonne* was taken into Edinburgh and Ryan, by now suspected to be the notorious Irish pirate, was transferred to Edinburgh Castle, charged with high treason and jailed to await extradition to London. The other Irish 'rebels' were also imprisoned while the Americans, French and other nationalities (who came from sovereign states that were 'officially' at war with Britain) were sent to be exchanged.

On 10 October 1781, Ryan and his first mate Thomas Coppinger were brought under heavy escort to London by road. They were presented at the Admiralty Sessions Court at the Old Bailey and charged with high treason and the piratical taking of vessels. When he came to trial in March 1782, Ryan still insisted on speaking French, even giving his name as 'Luc Ryan' and protesting that he was a naturalised citizen of King Louis and therefore liable to treatment as a *bona fide* prisoner of war.

However, nobody believed him, with one report in the London press wryly noting that while his French was awful, for an Irishman, he spoke English 'tolerably well'. As far as the British court was concerned, Luke Ryan was a British subject and therefore a traitor and a rebel. He would never be allowed to claim the protection of a foreign king, particularly when there was no documentary evidence that he had been offered or taken up French citizenship.

Any doubts about the identity of Ryan, who was still claiming to be a French officer, were dashed by the appearance of a string of witnesses from his native Rush, Co. Dublin, who testified to his real identity when he was eventually brought to trial. The witnesses who swore evidence included local land-owners, merchants some of his cousins and even fellow smugglers from Rush.

There would be payback for those from Rush who helped send Ryan to the gallows. In May 1782, Ryan's former officer and fellow Rush man Patrick Dowling returned home in the *Fear Not*.

Dowling landed with a large party of men at Skerries and burnt the houses of several witnesses against Ryan, including the home of the Revenue agent Frederick Connygham, in retaliation for the part they played in condemning their shipmates.

In London, Ryan and Coppinger had been charged with an eye-watering list of crimes, including mayhem, murder, mutiny, treason and piracy against George III. Ryan's defence was simple: he may indeed have carried out all of these acts, but he did so as a lawful privateer for the Americans and the French in a time of war. The Irishman was not likely to get a sympathetic hearing from the jury or from the notoriously hard Justice Sir James Marriott, a hanging judge if ever there was one.

While awaiting his fate, Ryan was joined at Newgate Prison by his former shipmate Edward Wilde of the *Black Princess* who had been captured off the Scillies. The Royal Navy had also apprehended the rest of Ryan's squadron, officers James Sweetman and Matthew Knight from Rush were also up for trial, and were convicted, in London in the summer of 1782.

Ryan's trial, in March 1782, effectively turned on his citizenship. If he could prove he was French he would go free. If he was found guilty of being Irish and a subject of King George, he would hang at Wapping.

There were witnesses for the defence who swore that Ryan was the French-born son of an officer serving in Dillon's Regiment in France and at one stage, they even produced a forged parish register from a little village in France which claimed to prove this. It was a touching story, the infant Luke had been brought to Rush to live with his relatives after the tragic death of his brave father in France. Justice Marriot was having none of it. Ryan was Irish and Ryan would hang. After three weeks (a lengthy trial for that period) the jury returned a verdict of guilty on all charges. His former shipmate and fellow Rush man, Thomas Coppinger, turned state's witness and earned himself a pardon. Edward Wilde (McCatter) and two other Dubliners, Nicholas Field of Skerries and Edward Duffy of Rush were convicted of piracy and treason along with Ryan.

On 14 May 1782, the four men (along with another officer, Thomas Farrell of the *Black Princess*) were sentenced to a particularly brutal form of execution and one that was meted out to the worst pirates of the era. They were to be 'caged' at Wapping on the London docks. Caging involved first partially strangling the condemned man before wrapping him in heavy chains and then locking him into a large iron cage that would be hung over the Thames river. As the tide rose, the cages would gradually slip beneath the water, drowning the condemned man even as he struggled for his last breath through the upper bars of his small prison.

The condemned men could appeal and were sent back to Newgate prison while the final legal formalities ran their course. At this stage, Ryan was joined in London by his wife and five children, who had lived in Rush through his career as a privateer.

Few could have held out hope for the Irishman. During a lengthy and legally arcane appeal process, he was ordered for execution four times, but was reprieved on each occasion. And Ryan still had one card to play.

Negotiations on ending the American Revolutionary War had begun and it seems Ryan still had some friends amongst the Americans and French, who began to put pressure on the British government to offer a pardon to Ryan. The British, who had been forced into a humiliating retreat from their US colonies and were anxious to normalise relations and get on with business, were mindful to hear these appeals. Lord Shelbourne, the Home Secretary, was instructed by the British cabinet to pardon Ryan, but execute one of the other pirates as 'an example to the others'. Ryan and his four officers would be pardoned, but an unfortunate Irish sailor called Daniel Casey, a first mate from the privateer fleet, would be caged at Wapping.

Hostilities between Britain, the United States and France formally ended on 27 February 1783 and Ryan was finally and formally pardoned and released on 9 February 1784. There had been a delay due to the significant legal debts Ryan had run up while defending his life and he had remained in Newgate Prison after his official pardon until the French government liquidated some of Torris's assets and sent funds to London to clear the lawyers' bills.

The war was over. But the spoils had still to be divided, and Ryan would now face a new fight to regain the money he had won during his brief, but spectacularly-successful, career. Now settled with his family in Hampshire, Ryan began legal action against his former agent in Dunkirk, Torris, and his bankers in Roscoff for over £70,000, a huge sum in the 1780s.

And then came one final twist in the story: the bankers claimed that a woman, who had presented herself as Ryan's 'wife', had called on them and claimed the Dubliner's fortune. As *The Gentleman's Magazine* of June 1789 reported, the bankers 'having trusted a woman passed on them as his wife, they 'suffered her to draw the whole out on his conviction, and she defrauded him of every shilling.' Whether this 'mystery woman', who was able to hoodwink a bank that was well accustomed to dealing with pirate money ever existed, we can only guess. Could she have been an ex-mistress? An agent of Torris or of one of his other associates? What is certain is that Ryan would never see his fortune.

The Dubliner was declared bankrupt in late 1788 and arrested on 25 February 1789 by the High Sheriff of Hampshire on foot of a debt of £200 owed to local doctors who had inoculated him and his family against smallpox, using the recently-developed Jenner method. Luke Ryan died in the King's Bench Debtors' Prison in London on 18 June 1789 of blood poisoning caused by an infected wound. He was one year short of his fortieth birthday.

Even then, there were some in France who claimed that Ryan had not died at all and that he had used one last trick to con the British authorities, escape to France and reclaim his fortune. It is a romantic notion. And one in keeping with the story of Luke Ryan.

The Obituary of Luke Ryan, from the *Gentleman's Magazine*
London, June 1789

In the King's Bench prison, Luke Ryan, captain of the *Black Prince* privateer during the war, who captured more vessels belonging to Great Britain than any other single ship during the war. The various scenes he went through are astonishing. He sailed from the port of Rush, in Ireland, early in the year 1778, in the *Friendship*, a smuggling cutter of eighteen six-pounders, whose name he afterwards changed to the *Black Prince*, and did more injury to the trade of these kingdoms than any single commander ever did. He was taken in 1781 by one of our ships of war, tried as a pirate at the Old Bailey, condemned, and four different times ordered for execution, but reprieved; and on peace being made, obtained his pardon through the Court of France. In 1781 he had realized near 20,000l. by his piracies, and lodged this sum in his bankers hands; but having trusted a woman passed on them as his wife, they suffered her to draw the whole out on his conviction, and she defrauded him of every shilling.

COLONEL WILLIAM
COTTER
AND THE MUNSTER FARMERS WHO
FOUGHT THE EMPEROR OF BRAZIL

We don't know much about Colonel William Cotter, beyond the fact that he was an Irish mercenary soldier without a conscience, a man who, in the early nineteenth century, conned more than two and a half thousand Cork and Waterford farmers into fighting for the Emperor of Brazil. In one of the more bizarre episodes in Irish history, Cotter, a soldier of fortune in the service of Emperor Dom Pedro I of Brazil, was responsible for luring the Irish men, women and children to South America with the promise of a new life. When they arrived, they discovered that, far from farming, they had been recruited to form an 'Irish Legion' to fight against Argentinean-backed rebels in the war of the 'Banda Oriental' in present-day Uruguay. In the end, the only fighting most of them saw was with German immigrants, African slaves and Imperial soldiers on the streets of Rio de Janeiro. The Irish-led rioting in the hot summer of 1828 left hundreds dead and a large part of Brazil's *Cidade Maravilhosa* – marvellous city – a smoking ruin; their murderous rampage, together with shattering naval victories won by a Mayo man fighting for the Argentine nation, helped to redraw the map of South

America. It's strange to think that for all of the violence and social upheaval it has seen, the single worst episode of communal violence ever to hit Rio was caused by a couple of thousand Munster farmers who took a wrong turn. Hundreds of them would never leave Rio again and would fall victim to violence, disease and destitution. Those who survived would be scattered to the four winds, ending up as refugees in Britain or in isolated pockets of South America and the West Indies.

Irish people travelled in their thousands to South America at the end of the eighteenth and start of the nineteenth centuries. Some found fame and considerable fortune, from the Irish who established rancher dynasties on the prairie-lands of Argentina to soldiers and statesmen like Admiral William Brown and Bernardo O'Higgins. But as well as these successes, there were also the 'forgotten' Irish of South America, mostly land-hungry Catholics looking for a better life. Under the Sugar Loaf of Rio de Janeiro in the late 1820s, some of these forgotten Irish men and women became known as *escravos brancos'* – the 'white slaves'.

The reasons for the 'white slaves' presence in Brazil date back several years to 1825. The newly-crowned emperor of Brazil, Dom Pedro I (who would become King of Portugal in 1826), was facing the dual problems of war with his Spanish-speaking, Argentine neighbours to the south along the border marked by the River Plate and dynastic battles with his relations amongst the ruling family of the mother country, Portugal.

The River Plate was a hotly-contested zone, where Portuguese Brazil and the former Spanish colonies of Argentina butted up against each other, with what is today Uruguay as the relatively-tiny piggy-in-the-middle. Pedro's father, King John VI, had crushed an earlier uprising by Argentine-backed, Spanish-speaking colonists in what the Portugese claimed as Cisplatine Province (formally the Banda Oriental, modern-day Uruguay). In 1825, the province was once again in rebellion and the Emperor of Brazil was facing defeat.

In the lingering turmoil of post-Napoleonic Europe, Dom Pedro was fighting to assert his right to the throne of faraway Portugal while striving to build an empire in the vast, fractious territories of Brazil. The Emperor's brother, Dom Miguel, had designs on both his thrones and their conflict would only be resolved after a major war that would end in a deal brokered by Britain, Spain and France and the exile of Dom Miguel. The war for the Banda Oriental – that land bordering Argentina and the River Plate to the south and Brazil to the north – had started well for Dom Pedro thanks to his largely Portuguese troops, hardened by years of fighting alongside the British (led by the Irish-born Duke of Wellington) in the brutal Peninsular War against Napoleon.

The Brazilians were fighting against ill-trained and irregular forces of Argentine *gauchos* who received little or no backing from the government in Buenos Aires. However, the long conflict had worn down the Brazilian forces and many of the Portuguese veterans had returned home, leaving native-born Brazilian soldiers from tropical regions to fight in, what was for them, a desolate and cold region. By early 1827, the war was not going well for Dom Pedro.

In addition to the problems on land, the Brazilian navy was being pressured by the Argentines, under the command of Mayo-born Admiral William Brown, one of the great heroes of Argentine history. Brown, already a legend of the Argentine war of independence, had long warned of the danger posed to Buenos Aires by the Brazilian navy, but had been ignored by the politicians who, forgetting the great service he had already done for their country, dismissed him as 'a foreigner'.

When the Brazilians began a menacing blockade of the Argentine coast, those same politicians came cap in hand to the Irish admiral and begged him to come out of retirement and organise a naval force.

Brown sprang into action and hastily pulled together a scratch squadron of ships; in early February 1827 he prepared to take on the Brazilian forces at the mouth of the Uruguay River, within cannon shot of the now fearful city of Buenos Aires. At the hard-fought Battle of Juncal at the mouth of the River Plate in February 1827, with just seven ships and eight single gun launches, Brown sank, took or disabled twelve of the opposing Brazilian squadron of seventeen ships. He also took its commander, Sena Pereira, prisoner. Before the battle, Brown addressed his officers and men, declaring 'Comrades: confidence in victory, discipline, and three hails to the motherland!' And as the Brazilian ships came within cannon shot, the indefatigable Mayo man shouted; 'Open fire, the people are watching us!' The then fifty-year-old Brown immediately went on the offensive after his first major victory, taking the war at sea to the Imperial navy of Dom Pedro I by attacking shipping and military targets along the Brazilian coast. After a further violent and decisive sea battle in June 1827, Brown had, against great odds, shattered the Brazilian navy and forced the Imperial forces to sue for peace. When the Irish admiral returned to Buenos Aires, he was greeted by bonfires and wild street celebrations from a relieved and thankful populace; the hard-fighting Irishman was a 'foreigner' no more.

Even before Brown's victory at sea over Brazil, Dom Pedro realised that the tide of the war had started to turn against him; with his navy and army under great pressure and a chronic lack of colonists from Portugal, Dom Pedro was running short of men and material, so he made plans to encourage European immigration and put a premium on tradesmen, farmers and mercenaries.

The Emperor needed soldiers. One war might shortly come to an uneasy peace, but he knew that there would be others. Also, Brazil was desperately short of the type of European colonists who could build up agriculture, industry and infrastructure. Dom Pedro believed his empire was stagnating, being left behind by the more energetic and expansion-minded Argentines to the south. An earlier influx of up to five thousand German emigrants, organised by Gregor von Schaffer, an unscrupulous German officer in the service of the Emperor, was halted after the various German governments became alarmed at the numbers leaving the Fatherland. Dom Pedro turned to the era's favoured source for cheap cannon-fodder and expendable colonists – the Irish.

Decades of poverty and persecution at home had pushed many thousands of Irishmen into the service of the great powers of Europe. There were four Irish Regiments fighting for the King of Spain, Napoleon had had his own *La Legion Irlandaise* and the Austrians, Swedes, Poles and, of course, British, all had significant Irish contingents in their armies. The Irish fought in the Seven Years' War in the mid-1700s (the first truly global war), the American War of Independence, with almost all the sides in the Napoleonic Wars and in India, South and North America, Africa and beyond.

Waterford-born Robert Walsh, a prominent anti-slavery activist, was chaplain to the British embassy in Rio at the time and later wrote that Dom Pedro decided on; 'the Irish, who from the redundancy of population at home, might be easily procured.'

William Cotter, an Irish-born colonel in the service of the Brazilian army, was despatched to Ireland in October 1826 to start the recruitment process.

He was recruiting on fertile ground. The Irish economy and population had expanded towards the end of the eighteenth century (the population was around five million by 1800) but from the start of the nineteenth century, the economy was in sharp decline.

The final defeat of Napoleonic France in 1813 brought disaster for Ireland's agricultural sector as Britain could once again look to the continent for grain and other food-stuffs. In the post-war period, prices paid for Irish grain fell by fifty-per cent, prices for butter by a third.

Irish farms were small and impoverished, there was a huge hunger for land from an expanding population (up to 6.8m by 1831) and rents were soaring as landlords squeezed every last drop from an increasingly-desperate people. In the mid-1820s, as Cotter was looking to recruit Irish families for the Emperor of Brazil, the wool and cotton manufacturing trade, which had been protected behind a wall of import duties, virtually collapsed, heaping further economic misery on the island.

Recent studies show that the average agricultural labourer of the time could expect to work only around half the days of the year. To a small farmer or labourer from Cork or Water-ford, this Irish gentleman-officer from Brazil, with his promise of free transport, free land and a new life in the New World, must have seemed like an emissary from heaven. Cotter sent out advertising bills across Munster, promising free passage, provisions (including clothes) and a grant of land in the exciting new country of Brazil for those brave enough to take the opportunity of a lifetime. Advertisements were placed in Irish newspapers and recruitment pitches were read out in churches and tacked to the walls of country courthouses. Ominously, a stipulation that some light military service might also be involved was relegated to the small print.

Many of the recruiting posters made no mention at all of possible service in the army of the Emperor of Brazil. Contemporary sources, like the British embassy chaplain Robert Walsh, say that many of the men who signed up understood that there would be an obligation to train as militiamen to defend their settlements while others 'whose idle habits led them to prefer a military life', freely volunteered for the army. Walsh, who interviewed many of his fellow Irishmen in Rio shortly after the uprising, recorded that many of them had hoped to find a new life in Brazil.

'The notifications were received with great joy by the people,' Walsh recorded in his *Notices of Brazil* in 1828 and 1829, published in London shortly after his return from South America.

'The exceeding distress of the poor peasantry of that part of Ireland, as well from exuberant population as want of employment, is notorious, and they were eager to avail themselves of the proposal.

'Land was the great object of their competition at home, and they who thought themselves fortunate in obtaining a few acres at an exorbitant rent in Ireland, were transported at the idea of receiving a grant of fifty acres, rent free, in Brazil.

'Many, therefore, as they told me, sold their farms at home, and laid out the small portion of money they could raise, in purchasing agricultural implements, conceiving that their military service was to be merely local, and would no more prevent their attending to their land, than if they were members of yeomanry corps in their own country.

'Some of them, as was to be expected, were of indifferent characters and dissolute manners; but the majority decent, respectable people, who brought out with them their wives and families, and who would be an acquisition to any country as settlers, but particularly to Brazil.'

Colonel William Cotter was a natural-born salesman and quickly signed up between 2,400 and 2,500 farmers and their families, almost none of whom had military experience of any kind. A small armada of ten ships would eventually set sail from Cork to Brazil (for the ports of Rio, Espirito Santo and Sao Paulo) carrying a total of 3,169 passengers, comprising 2,450 men, 335 women, 123 young boys and girls and 230 children.

One ship, the *Charlotte Maria*, left Cork on 9 September 1827 with two hundred and fifty men, twenty-six women, and nine children on board, arriving in Rio de Janeiro 22 December.

A man called William Herbert, perhaps sensing which way the wind was blowing, jumped ship in Tenerife. Thirteen died on board and of the other families, familiar Irish names like Welsh, Leahy, Maher, Hartnett, Daly, McCarthy, O'Leary, Sullivan, Power, Mills and O'Shea were recorded in the ship's manifest. The contracts they had signed (even if, in many cases, not fully understood) promised them pay and allowances equal to one shilling per day plus victuals, as well as a grant of forty acres of land after five years of service to the Emperor. The key point was that their military service would be limited to four hours of training each day and while they would be ready to act as a kind of army reserve, the Irish would 'not be sent out of the province of Rio unless in time of war or invasion'. They did not know of the bitter, intermittent and drawn-out war that was already being fought on the disputed border between Argentina and Brazil. The Irish settlers arrived in Rio de Janeiro between December 1827 and January 1828. They were arriving into a city already seething with resentment against the 'Irish mercenaries' brought across the sea to fight a deeply-unpopular and virtually-lost war. And to add further to the confusion and ill-feeling – that war had largely fizzled out. The British had mediated a conclusion that saw the disputed Cisplatine Province gain its independence as Uruguay.

However, it seemed the Emperor still wanted his Irish soldiers. There would be other wars. And Dom Pedro's ambitions and jealousies, his thwarted efforts to seize the region around the River Plate, had been draining Brazil of men and resources. There was little goodwill towards the impoverished Irish, the blow-ins who would be competing for land, jobs, shelter and food in the teeming streets of Rio and the poorly-developed fields beyond.

Brazilian newspapers, politicians and businessmen opposed to the war against the Argentines to the south had poisoned local opinion against the Irish. The German soldiers and settlers who had preceded them were already pariahs in the city and had fought running battles in the streets with the nativists and African slaves.

One English resident of Rio recorded the sight of the bedraggled Irish landing on, what must have been for peasant farmers from Waterford and Cork, a very foreign shore: 'Mothers with their infants at their breast, young girls approaching womanhood, and athletic labourers in the prime of life were all landed in a state of almost utter nudity'.

Almost as soon as the gang-planks had lowered, the Irish settlers discovered that Colonel William Cotter had sold them a pack of lies. The agents of Dom Pedro tried immediately to press-gang them into regiments to serve their four or five years as his soldiers, ready to be sent South or to whatever region the Emperor's ambitions took him next.

In the uneasy, confused times immediately after the disastrous loss of her province and navy to Argentina and the rebels, the just-arrived Irish were plunged into the simmering tensions and resentments of an empire in deep trouble. Their women and children would have been left stranded on the docks and William Cotter, their only mediator with the Brazilian authorities, was nowhere to be seen. We can imagine the scenes: families separated, sergeants trying to march uncomprehending Irishmen off to their barracks, their hopes for a new life in a new land dashed within hours of arriving after a harrowing sea voyage.

After much confusion, the Irish were marched between files of local militia to the barracks at Barbonos Street 'amid the taunts of the populace and the jeers of multitudes of negroes, shouting and clapping their hands at the unexpected apparition of the "white slaves", as they pleased to denominate the unfortunate Irish', according to Chaplain Walsh.

After a welcome like that, William Cotter's promises of great opportunities in a new land of plenty must have started to ring hollow. When they reached the overcrowded, squalid barracks, they found that their living quarters and food fell far short of the standard promised by William Cotter. Their new life in Brazil had started badly and it was about to get a lot worse.

Although some were ready to serve the Emperor, many of the Irish, who had thought they would merely be joining farmer's militias, violently resisted attempts to put them into the imperial army uniform and sought help from the British ambassador, Robert Gordon.

Gordon was an 'ill-mannered and obstinate Scot' in the view of Dom Pedro, but the British minister in Rio knew his duty and Dom Pedro was dependent on British goodwill for his plans for both Brazil and Portugal.

Gordon immediately lodged a strongly-worded protest with the Brazilian court and after further pressure from the British, the Imperial Army backed down on plans to press-gang every Munsterman who could shoulder a musket.

Fewer than four hundred Irishmen eventually joined the Imperial Army and any plans for creating an Irish Legion had to be abandoned. As they were too few to become a separate unit, the Irishmen were integrated into the Third (German) Battalion of Grenadiers and found themselves sharing the ranks with that equally-disgruntled band of recent arrivals who didn't speak their language.

The war on the Argentine frontier was all but over, thanks largely to their countryman William Brown and his destruction of Brazilian naval forces, so the Irish who did sign up never made it to the front. The Munster settlers were now stranded in Rio with no real protectors and little or no help from the authorities who no longer needed them to fight their war. They lived in squalid, disease-ridden barracks and shacks and depended on the help of two British doctors, Dixon and Coates, for medicines and food relief.

The enslaved Africans – called '*moleques*' – were in the majority in the capital, and they had their reasons for harbouring a violent antipathy towards the Irish and German settlers and mercenaries. As the poorest class of people in Brazil, the *moleques* took a 'fiendish delight in tormenting the destitute Irish', according to the Irish-born churchman Robert Walsh, brawling with the 'white slaves' in the street. Abandoned, starving and unarmed, the Munstermen responded by forming ad hoc street gangs and fighting the Africans with sticks and stones through the back alleys of Rio.

After six months of escalating tensions, the Brazilian government, under increasing pressure from the British and concerned about the gangs of Irish who were now threatening civil order, started to look for ways to ship them out. Colonel William Cotter made a brief reappearance on the scene, charged with chastising his rebellious Irish recruits, but his presence only served to inflame the Irish migrants who felt they had been cheated and lied to. Cotter was lucky to escape with his life.

On 15 March 1828, 101 families of Cork and Waterford emigrants left Rio on the *Victoria* for Salvador, a town further up the Atlantic coast of Brazil. They arrived in early August and settled as farm labourers in Taperoa, near Valença. Some struggled on to build a new life for themselves, others kept travelling northwards towards the United States. In June, the remaining eighty or so Irish serving in the Grenadier Battalion decided to join a large band of their German comrades in a violent mutiny: on the morning of 11 June a party of fourteen mutinous German grenadiers left their barracks at Sao Cristovao to capture their hated Brazilian commander on the streets of Rio. The Brazilian major, tipped off to their approach, managed to barricade himself into a police station. The Germans stormed the police station, but the major escaped on a fast horse. The mutineers were spotted by a party of up to eighty Irish soldiers and the two forces joined up and started rampaging through the streets of downtown Rio. Their ranks swelled by Irish and German civilians, the mob started looting shops and bars, burning houses and terrorising the indigenous poor people of Rio, the *cariocas*. The Irish mob included women and children, who, according to reports given shortly after the riots, helped to burn up to a hundred houses and businesses, killing or maiming many of the occupants.

The situation soon descended into outright anarchy, within hours, ferocious street battles involving the Munstermen, Germans, local militias and black African slaves had erupted across Rio. The Irish soldiers and their families raged through the streets, shouting 'Death to the Brazilians!' and 'Death to the Portuguese!'

The fact that Rio was home to countless shebeens and hostelries, all selling cheap, potent rum and other local spirits, did not help to calm the situation. Many of the Irish and Germans were said to be fuelled by stolen alcohol and there were reports that some dropped dead through the combination of intense heat, exertion and rum.

At the height of the battle, the Emperor's Minister of War, Barroso responded by telling his troops, 'Kill them all. Give no quarter to anybody. Kill those foreigners!'

Some Irish civilians and soldiers did hold back from the rampage; at Praia Vermelha, today the popular 'Red Beach' of Rio, underneath the Sugar Loaf mountain, an officer called Colonel MacGregor managed to restrain his Irish/German infantry battalion, but he could not persuade his men to help put down the rioting and the battalion stayed out of the street battles that went on through the night and into the following days.

The Irish from the Third Battalion took the lead in the rioting and went after Colonel Cotter. After months of hardship and lies, they wanted a reckoning with the Irish soldier of fortune they accused of selling them into slavery. The mob chased Cotter and his officers out of the Campo de Santana area of downtown Rio and attacked a police post, killing six policemen.

Large parts of Rio were now in flames. The entire city was in uproar. There was a real danger that the Irish and German mutineers and rioters could overrun the Imperial Palace.

In total desperation, the authorities issued arms to the civilian population, including the slaves. This was an unprecedented measure and a clear indication of how worried the civil and military authorities had become. After all, there was no guarantee that the black slaves would not seize the chance to throw in their lot with the *brancos* against their common masters.

For the first time ever, the African population of Rio was allowed to practise their secret *capoeira* martial art on the streets as they went up against the Irish mob that was armed with muskets, sticks, stones, machetes and bottles. After forty-eight hours of pitched battles, the heavily-outnumbered and exhausted Munstermen withdrew to their barracks and barricaded themselves in.

There was a pause in the street battles and reports talk of an eerie calm settling over the ruined streets of Rio. It was not to last long.

Brazilian troops were rushed to the capital and Dom Pedro appealed to local British and French naval commanders to land sailors and marines to help them. On 12 and 13 June, the rebel barracks were put under siege by a multinational, multi-coloured force of slaves, soldiers, sailors and marines. British and French forces, stationed on ships in the harbour, had agreed to act as holding troops at strategic points around the city to allow Imperial forces to be freed up to take on the Irish and Germans.

The mutineers and their families were given one last chance to surrender. Some did, but many decided to fight to the end. The episode ended in carnage, with as many as a hundred and fifty soldiers of fortune, both German and Irish, killed during the mutiny. Hundreds of Brazilian soldiers and hundreds more local civilians also died. The exact figures are not recorded. The heat and confusion led to many bodies simply being tipped into unmarked, communal graves across Rio. The surviving Irish and German mutineers were marched through the streets, back to the harbour where they had arrived earlier that year, and crammed into disease-ridden prison hulks. By this stage, Emperor Dom Pedro was desperate to rid himself of his rebellious Munster subjects and in July 1828 and with the help of the British, arranged for around 1,400 of the immigrants to be put on boats for Ireland and Britain. Perhaps as many as four hundred other Irish remained in Brazil as farmers and eventually settled in the southern provinces of Santa Catarina and Rio Grande do Sul. This leaves some six hundred Irish immigrants unaccounted for, most of whom probably met their death in Rio, in the surrounding regions or on ships bound for some sort of sanctuary. The emperor Dom Pedro blamed the entire incident on the minister for war, Barroso, whom he accused of inciting the mutiny and doing nothing to suppress it.

This was a mite unfair to Minister Barroso, as he had unleashed the Imperial Troops with the order, 'Kill every foreigner!'

However, such were the tensions and rivalries within Pedro's court, with one eye always on potential dynastic rivals from Portugal, that Pedro undoubtably needed a fall-guy and the Minister, who had been involved in the disasterous war with Argentina, was it.

Large parts of Rio were devastated, hundreds were dead and mutilated bodies littered the streets.

The Emperor's best regiments had been battered by the mutineers and his plans to bring thousands more settlers from Ireland were in ruins (by this stage, the Emperor could be forgiven for never wanting to hear a Munster accent again).

His forces, assaulted on land by Irish farmers-turned-mutineers and on sea by their countryman Admiral Brown, were in a disastrous state.

Dom Pedro was soon forced into a humiliating and costly concession to the French, who were demanding (with menaces) compensation for ships and cargoes blockaded in Rio harbour during the Napoleonic wars. Dom Pedro's gamble on Irish and German mercenaries and his trust in unscrupulous men like Colonel William Cotter had back-fired in grand style. There are no further accounts of Colonel William Cotter in Brazilian history. However, there is a mention of a 'Colonel Cotter' taking part in a military expedition to Portugal on behalf of Dom Pedro in 1832, during one episode of the inter-minable dynastic struggles involving the Portuguese aristocracy.

The report, by a British-born officer in the service of Dom Pedro, a Colonel G. Lloyd Hodges, mentions a recent arrival of 'British troops' under the command of Colonel Cotter and complains that these troops are 'almost naked and shoeless' and in no condition to fight.

Could these 'British troops' be a remnant of the Irishmen brought by Cotter to Brazil? The fact that they are destitute and Colonel William Cotter is involved, would lead us to conclude that at the very least, William Cotter had not changed his *modus operandi*.

Even in this detailed record of the campaign, Cotter slips, once again out of the story, just as he slipped out of the story of the Munster men, women and children he caused to be scattered to the four winds.

In the style befitting the man, he disappeared from the story, almost certainly weighed down with a large commission for selling out his countrymen.

SIR HUGH GOUGH
LIMERICK'S OPIUM WARLORD

It is hardly an honour for Limerick, but the Treaty City can lay claim to the most ruthless, brutal and successful drug lord in history. And also the most decorated and respected.

Sir Hugh Gough was much more than just a mid-nineteenth century Pablo Escobar. While modern international criminals work in the shadows, Sir Hugh had the blessing of Queen Victoria and her government and operated with flags flying and marching bands playing. And unlike the Mexican cartels or the Colombian cocaine Kings, Sir Hugh and his backers thought big. China big. It was globalisation by gun-boat and nothing less than the deliberate enslaving of millions of people to drug addiction and the ruin of an ancient empire for profit.

It seems incredible to us now that a military and commercial superpower would fight a major war to force a country the size of China to accept a massive and officially-sanctioned narcotics trade. But, in the mid-nineteenth century, that is exactly what the British did. In fact, they fought two wars for the right to trade in narcotics, what became known as the Opium Wars. And Limerick's General, Sir Hugh Gough, commanded the British forces in the first. It would result in humiliation and degradation for an ancient kingdom and a treaty that including the ceding of Hong Kong as a long-term British trading base.

The aim of the British commercial interests in 1839 was to force the Heavenly Middle Kingdom, the Empire of China, to allow annual shipments of tonnes of narcotics, brought from British-controlled India. By the end of the 1830s, the trade had been going on, illicitly or with the collusion of local and regional Chinese officials, for decades. In 1820, to take one year, some nine hundred tonnes of Indian opium were brought by British trading ships of the East India Company to China. And by the height of the trade there were an estimated twelve million addicts.

As well as narcotics, the British (along with the French and other colonial powers) also wanted to force the Chinese to open their vast markets up to European textiles, technology and trade goods, while emptying their treasuries to pay. Then, as today, there was a trade imbalance between East and West. Europeans wanted Chinese goods – everything from porcelain and silk to tea. However, the Chinese imperial rulers were steadfastly refusing to open up their markets to the outsiders and the gold and silver only went one way. In the mid-nineteenth century, guns and drugs were the means by which the scales would be balanced.

And when the Chinese tried to resist the opium trade and push back against European commercial rapacity, Sir Hugh Gough's forces were the hammer that would smash all resistance and open up the vast kingdom to the hugely-profitable imperial British drug trade at the point of a cannon; British flintlocks and Royal Navy gunboats (an innovation of the Opium Wars) would clear the road for British commerce.

It was clear what the motives were for conflict with China and not everybody amongst the British ruling elite supported the cause.

At the conclusion of the First Opium War in 1842, a newly-elected MP called William Ewart Gladstone (who would go on to be one of the greatest statesmen of the age) asked if there had ever been 'a war more unjust in its origin, a war more calculated to cover this country with permanent disgrace.' However, the then Foreign Secretary, Lord Palmerston, put the upstart MP in his place by pointing out that nobody 'could say that he honestly believed the motive of the Chinese Government to have been the promotion of moral habits' and declared that the war was merely a trade dispute, fought to stem China's balance of payments deficit.

There was profit to be had and it made economic sense. Britain had access to vast stocks of opium in the Indian subcontinent. The opium would right the trade imbalance, Chinese gold and silver would flow out of the Heavenly Middle Kingdom and the trade barriers that blocked European goods from a potentially massive market would fall.

There was also an empire to be built. Gough's dirty war would lead directly to the founding of Hong Kong, the cornerstone of British commerce in the Far East for a century and a half. For the Chinese, it would result in the military humiliation and eventual disintegration of an ancient empire. They still call it their 'Century of Humiliation'. It meant the addiction of millions of Chinese people, of all walks to life, to opium, and also led to decades of decay and economic and political chaos, what the Chinese call '*Hundun*' or 'primordial chaos', from which the country has only recently (in historic terms, at least) started to emerge.

The British historian Niall Ferguson has recently argued that *Hundun* is at the root of the current Chinese regime's almost paranoid need for the total control of all aspects of political, social and intellectual life.

Limerick's Sir Hugh Gough may have only been the instrument of ruthless international trade, one of the many soldiers at the sharp end of the vast colonial and commercial project, however, if the Chinese have good reason to hold a grudge against the British, there must be a small part of the national psyche that still remembers a son of Limerick with a special hatred.

Hugh Gough was a son of solid Anglo-Irish stock, born on the outskirts of Limerick City on 3 November 1779. His forebears were pillars of the Anglo-Irish community from their arrival in Ireland during the reign of King James I, counting bishops, barristers, High Sheriffs and militia colonels amongst their number. Sir Hugh's father was Lieutenant Colonel George Gough, who commanded the Limerick City militia in putting down the local United Irishmen of the 1798 rebellion and fought the French and Irish forces at Westport and Johnstown.

Hugh, one of six children of George Gough and Letitia Bunbury, won his commission into the British army at the age of thirteen and began a military career that was to last most of his life and be blessed by spectacular successes. Two of his brothers were also very successful soldiers, one, William, fought at the Battle of Salamanca in the Peninsular War and was later badly wounded at Vittoria. He was drowned off the Old Head of Kinsale in 1822 (along with hundreds of others) while returning from North America on board the passenger ship *Albion*.

Sir Hugh was said never to have lost a significant battle, he won four colonial wars and commanded at more major engagements than any other British officer of the nineteenth century bar the Duke of Wellington, victor of Waterloo. As one biographer noted, Sir Hugh was 'nurtured amidst the clash of arms', spending his formative years hearing the tales of father's Limerick militia as they taught the local Croppies to lie down.

Gough's military career would take him all over the world, fighting for the interests of the British Empire in Spain, Portugal, Africa, the West Indies, India and China. He was brave, often to the point of recklessness, leading almost always from the front and usually limiting his tactics to the shock and awe of frontal assault, especially against less well-trained and well-armed 'native' forces. Military historians and his contemporary generals have tended to dismiss Gough (perhaps unfairly given his record) as a poor strate-gist and inept tactician. However, Napoleon was famously said to have asked of any officer he was considering of promoting to general, 'Is he lucky?' And in the case of Sir Hugh Gough, who fought and routed *l'Empereur*'s forces in the Peninsular Wars, the answer would have been very much in the affirmative. In an age when military commanders were supposed to have dash, *élan* and an almost insane disregard for their own personal safety, Sir Hugh Gough and his enormous mutton-chops would always be front and centre in the line of battle, showing a steely contempt for the perils of the battlefield.

At the Battle of Sobraon in 1846, during the First Sikh War, when told that his troops were running short of ammunition, Sir Hugh was heard to mutter, 'Thank God! Then I'll be at them with the bayonet.' He survived horses being shot out from under him and bullet wounds in Portugal, shrapnel tearing through his uniform in India and the best efforts of opposing armies on three continents. During the Battle of Ferozeshan, again in the First Sikh War, his infantry was being mown down in rows by heavy cannon fire (the British had trained the Sikhs, ferocious fighters they valued as a 'martial race', as expert gunners). Gough, deciding he needed a diversion to draw the enemy fire away from his troops, began galloping across the enemy front, dressed in his famous white 'fighting coat.' The Sikh gunners recognised the General, opened fire and missed. Gough won the battle. It was hardly a textbook stratagem, but it was in keeping with his general 'Have at 'em, lads!' approach to warfare.

It was war and it was often bloody slaughter. And if that meant suppressing slave rebellions in the West Indies, putting thousands of 'rebellious' Sikhs to the sword (in their own country) or forcing opium down the throats of the Chinese at the point of a twenty-four-inch bayonet, Sir Hugh had his orders and he wasn't going to let sentiment get in the way.

His long, varied and world-ranging military career (including duty in Ireland in 1829 suppressing outrages) reflected the global ambitions of the rapidly-expanding British Empire from the end of the eighteenth century onwards. As a young officer he served with the 78th Highland regiment during their capture of the Cape of Good Hope and the Dutch Fleet in 1795. Gough then served in the West Indies, fighting against the French and helping to put down slave uprisings on the island of St Lucia (slavery continued in the British colonies of the West Indies until 1838) along with the Irishmen of the 87th Royal Irish Fusiliers under General Sir John Doyle.

It was during Wellington's campaigns against Napoleon in the Peninsular Wars that Gough really came into his own, fighting with the 87th (the Prince of Wales' Irish Regiment, also known as the 'Faugh a Ballaghs' for their ancient Gaelic war cry). Nelson had won at Trafalgar, but Napoleon's armies had decimated the Austrians and Russians at Austerlitz and the British recognised the Iberian peninsular as the soft underbelly of the French empire.

Sir Hugh came to the attention of Wellington for his bravery at the battle of Talavera, where he was severely wounded after having his horse shot out from under him. The Iron Duke recommended his immediate promotion to Lieutenant Colonel. It's unlikely that Wellington would have been even partly motivated by their shared Irish heritage; the Iron Duke may well have been born on Merrion Street in Dublin, but as he himself said of his unwanted

Irish ancestry; 'Being born in a stable does not make one a horse'.

Gough was a popular figure amongst the ruling classes of Ireland in the high Victorian period, a highly-decorated, martial hero of the Empire. In a popular romantic novel of the 1880s, *Diana of the Crossways,* the author George Meredith describes a grand society ball in Dublin to 'celebrate the return to Erin of a British hero of Irish blood, after his victorious campaign in India; a mighty struggle splendidly ended'. Meredith's pen picture of the General, 'a fine old warrior, tall, straight, grey-haired, martial in his aspect and decorations' was based directly on Gough, a hero of the age having added the Punjab to Queen Victoria's Empire. The Peninsular Wars had made him and his Indian campaigns were the crown on his career. But it was China that would confirm Gough as one of the most successful soldiers of his era.

The First Opium War (1839-1842) was the inevitable result of decades of growing tensions between European colonial interests and the weak and isolated Qing Dynasty of China.

Direct trade between Europe and China had started in the mid-sixteenth century when the far-ranging Portuguese had established a trading post in Macau.

From 1556 onwards, the Spanish, with their colonies in the Philippines, started a global trade that brought silver from the mines of South America to the Far East and saw silks, tea, porcelain and other goods travel in the other direction to Europe.

It was the beginnings of globalisation – some four centuries before the term was coined.

However, the Spanish were facing a major trade imbalance. European markets were hungry for Chinese goods, but the Chinese, who effectively locked down their kingdom from the influences and products of outside 'barbarians', were not interested in anything the Spanish had to offer beyond precious metals.

So the Spanish traders hit on new trade goods, chiefly opium, as a means of reversing the one-way flow of silver.

For the Spanish, and much more so for their successors as masters of global trade, the British, opium was the perfect solution to the age old trade deficit with China. Opium was cheap and easy to produce, coming from British-controlled lands in the Indian subcontinent. And millions of loyal, addicted customers would reverse the flow of silver from East to West.

The Chinese had developed a taste for opium, but remained very wary, at government level at least, of trade with the barbarians from the West and successive emperors tried various means to halt the spread of western trade, technology and influence in the Heavenly Middle Kingdom. By the middle of the eighteenth century, it was the globally-ascendant British, through the immensely powerful British East India Company, with a royal charter to trade with China, who began to dominate.

The Company could use private armies and navies to snuff out opposition (such as the French and Spanish) and keep reluctant regional rulers in line. The trade was gradually formalised into the Canton System, with the Europeans only allowed to trade through strictly controlled treaty ports of Zhoushan, Xiamen and

Guangzhou (Canton).

Tea exports from China to Britain alone grew from 92,000 pounds in 1700 to 2.7 million pounds in 1751. By 1800, the East India Company was buying twenty-three million pounds of tea per year, at a cost of 3.6 million pounds of silver; the Chinese would only accept payment in silver, the hard currency of the period. This put the British, who were on the gold standard, at a particular disadvantage as they had to buy silver from other European powers and Mexico to pay the Chinese. The British needed to find a trade good that was easy to source and produce, easy to transport and prove to be as irresistible to the Chinese as tea was to them. So in the early eighteenth century, despite vehement protests from the Qing rulers, British traders began importing opium from India.

For the British, it was the perfect, logical solution to a serious trade problem.

The Chinese ruling and intellectual elite was horrified and began a long and unsuccessful campaign to ban the narcotic that was turning vast numbers of their people into addicts. Emperor Yongzheng had banned the sale and smoking of opium as early as 1729 (small amounts were allowed to be imported for medicinal use). As the scale of illegal smuggling and selling increased, desperate officials made the trafficking of opium punishable by death. But as many governments since have found, prohibition and crackdowns, no matter how severe, have little to no effect on the distribution and consumption of drugs. Especially if that trade is enthusiastically sanctioned by the most powerful nation on the planet and backed by fleets of warships.

The opium trade multiplied, the narcotic came by the tonne from Bengal in the holds of British Indiamen (the East India Company had been granted a monopoly on the trade by the British crown) while the silver reserves of China went west. And the Chinese rulers were powerless to stop it.

The Qing government, isolated in Beijing, could not control the southern ports. By the 1820s, China was importing nine hundred tonnes of Bengali opium every year. There were an estimated twelve million addicts. It meant untold human misery, the dire weakening of industry, trade and agriculture and of the beggaring of an Empire.

In March 1839, the Chinese reached their breaking point. One of the Emperor's own sons had died from an overdose. An official called Lin Tse-Hsu was despatched to Canton to shut down the opium trade. When the British merchants refused to co-operate, Lin Tse-Hsu ordered the forcible seizing of opium supplies in the Cantons and the boarding of British ships bound for the treaty ports. Lin, regarded as an official of great integrity and energy by the Emperor Daoguang (or Tao-kuang as he was known in the West) had previously set up addiction treatment centres around the areas worst affected by opium addiction. Mindful of the powerful financial interests in the opium trade in London, the Qing government, through Lin Tse-Hsu, took the highly-unusual step of publishing an open letter to Queen Victoria, appealing to her moral judgement and asking how her country could profit from such as terrible trade (Queen Victoria herself was one of many British people who regularly used opium as a medicinal aid, it was not illegal in Great Britain at the time, but there was not a problem with widespread, chronic addiction).

The letter stated, 'Your Majesty has not before been thus officially notified, and you may plead ignorance of the severity of our laws, but I now give my assurance that we mean to cut this harmful drug forever.'

Foreign merchants and their goods were seized. Lin warned them that until they agreed to stop the illegal smuggling of opium, and sign binding agreements that they would never engage in the trade again, their goods, ships and persons were effectively hostages of the Chinese government. Until the opium trade stopped, all trade in tea, silk, rice and other items was prohibited, a move that would have meant financial disaster for British commercial interests. That was enough for the British East India Company, the Government and the money men in the City of London. After a series of skirmishes at sea involving local British squadrons and some diplomatic playing for time by the Chinese, a large British Indian Army and naval force was despatched to southern China in June 1840.

The British Foreign Secretary, Lord Palmerston, made no secret of the reason for this latest imperial war, it would be conducted to force the Chinese to pay full compensation for the opium destroyed on the orders of the Emperor. Public opinion in the United States, many parts of Europe and even in the United

Kingdom was outraged by what the young MP William Ewart Gladstone condemned in Parliament as this 'unjust and iniquitous' war, carried out to 'protect an infamous and contraband traffic'.

After some initial confusion over who would be best to command the force, it fell to Limerick's Sir Hugh Gough to hold overall command of the army, working with naval commander, Rear Admiral George Elliot. The force comprised almost five thousand men and seventy-three ships (including two seventy-four-gun ships-of-the-line, the aircraft carriers of their day). The plan of campaign was relatively simple, destroy the coastal fortifications, take or burn the Chinese junks that stood in their way and storm upriver, burning and looting as they went until the Chinese rulers had got the message. The battleships could destroy any fortifications, anchoring in front of the mud-brick forts and blazing away with twenty-eight thirty-two or thirty-six pound guns on the lower gun deck, thirty eighteen-pounders on the upper gun deck, and sixteen nine-pounders on the upper works.

However, powerful though the ships of the line were, Gough's secret weapon was the gunboat, developed specifically to navigate the shallow rivers of Southern China. These lethal, highly-manoeuvrable and heavily-armed steam-paddle boats could literally run rings around the slow-sailing Chinese ships and close in on any coastal or river defences. The most famous of these lethal paddle steamers was the *Nemesis*, called the 'Nevermiss' by the British sailors and 'Fire Devil' by the Chinese. *Nemesis* and her class could manoeuvre at eight knots in either direction and were loaded almost to the gunwales with cannon, primitive rockets and swivel guns. The Chinese forces were heavily outclassed; China had not had a national navy for centuries and their guns were primitive and totally ineffective against the state of the art British men–o–war. The British grand plan was to capture the coastal cities at the mouth of the Yangtze River, sail upwards towards the strategically-vital Grand Canal and blockade it, thus denying the critically-important food supply from southern China to the capital Peking (Beijing) in the North.

There were no major set-battles, the boats battered the coastal forts and cities, Gough and his commanders stormed ashore where needed, and the overwhelmed Chinese commanders were either paralysed with indecision or in headlong retreat. Gough was notoriously aggressive, favouring the mailed fist over complicated manoeuvres. The campaign progressed without any serious losses for the British. In one action at Canton, an enemy force of four thousand men was routed without the loss of a single man under Gough. In fact, the worst enemy the expeditionary force faced was disease, most notably dysentery.

In a slow, methodical campaign, the port of Canton was besieged and one by one, the coastal cities and strong-points along the Yangtze fell to the British tactics.

On 26 January 1841, a separate force under Commodore Gordon Brenner led a contingent of naval men ashore at Hong Kong to claim the lightly-defended island for Britain – it would remain in British hands until 1997.

In late February, Captain Charles Elliot (brother to the Admiral in command) successfully attacked the Bogue forts at Humen, took control of the Pearl River and laid siege to Canton. He only withdrew in May 1841 after extracting several tonnes of silver and other concessions from the merchants of Canton. By August 1841, an even larger British force sailed north and seized Amoy, Ningpo, Shanghai and other ports. With Nanjing under immediate threat, their forces in total disarray and the spectre of famine in Beijing looming over them, the Chinese sued for peace and accepted the Treaty of Nanjing in August, 1842. The Treaty of Nanjing was signed onboard a British warship by two Manchu imperial commissioners and the British plenipotentiary. It was the first of a series of agreements with the Western trading nations, later called by the Chinese the 'Unequal Treaties.'

The Treaty officially ceded the Island of Hong Kong to Britain 'in perpetuity' (Hong Kong would go on to become the British Empire's great commercial hub in the Far East, before being returned to the Chinese at the close of the twentieth century). Though from Gough's time onwards, there was growing opposition towards the opium trade – one MP, speaking in the 1880s, said that 'for every soul our missionaries sent to Heaven from China, the British Government was sending ten to hell by this traffic' – even up to the end of the First World War, Hong Kong, in particular, was addicted to the narcotics trade. In 1918, half the total revenue for the colony came from selling opium to China.

The treaty also opened up a series of ports along the Chinese coast to European trade, with Europeans for the first time being allowed to live freely within those ports, rather than in the strictly quarantined trade compounds of the past. The British and other European trading nations now had effectively free rein to open up China to their trade, very much on their terms.

The opium trade would soon resume; in 1858 the Chinese government accepted their country's fate and reluctantly legalised the importation of opium. As a final insult, they also agreed to pay huge indemnities, partly to cover the cost of the British-owned opium destroyed at the start of the war.

For the Chinese, it was the start of what they would call a century of 'national humiliations', more foreign incursions, forced trade, domestic chaos and the ever-present blight of opium.

For Limerick's General Sir Hugh Gough, China was just another campaign in a far-flung, exotic corner of the world.

He got his rewards, was created a baronet in December 1842 and soon after appointed C-in-C of British forces in India (where his bluff, soldierly ways would cause great friction with the civilian rulers of the Raj). The top job in India had been a long-term ambition for Gough, he had hoped for a relatively quiet life for himself and Lady Gough (his second wife) in the cool hill stations after a lifetime campaigning around the globe. Gough's war to secure the opium trade for British commercial interests had won him India. He was further elevated to the peerage in 1846, created Baron Gough of Chiang Kang Fu, before fresh war in India in 1848 saw him take the field again, fighting the Sikhs at the spectacularly bloody battle of Chillianwala.

His controversial tactics, which resulted in carnage on both sides, and the stalemate that followed, saw him recalled and replaced, but in another example of the luck that seemed to follow Gough through a lifetime of battle, he managed to defeat the Sikhs at the battle of Gujarat in early 1849, just before his replacement arrived.

Gough could now return home, as always, the conquering hero. He had first joined the British army fifty-six years previously. Gough would not fight again, he was voted a pension of £2,000 a year by the British Parliament (the grateful East India Company matched this) and he retired to a peaceful life with his family in Ireland. He died at Booterstown in Dublin in March 1869, in his ninetieth year in the palatial family home then known as St Helen's, today a landmark, five-star Radisson Hotel.

The grand entrance way to the hotel still displays a full-length portrait of the old soldier, with an Indian native bowed down at his side in supplication. The building also displays the motto '*Mors Potior Macula*' or 'Death rather than infamy'.

Gough was buried in Dublin and an equestrian statue of him was erected in the Phoenix Park. It was later vandalised and moved to England. He was also commemorated by Mount Gough on Hong Kong island, which is now back in the hands of the Chinese.

In tribute to the old soldier, the man sent out to replace him in India, Sir Charles Napier said, 'I like that noble old fellow Gough more than ever. Let me express my delight with old Gough; he is so good, so honest, so noble-minded.'

ALEJANDRO 'BLOODY' O'REILLY
DESPOT, EXECUTIONER, MEATH MAN.

Count Alexander O'Reilly, born into the remnants of the Irish Catholic aristocracy in Meath in 1723, fought in the armies of Spain, France and Austria during an extraordinary career that saw him campaign across Europe, the Caribbean, North Africa and the Spanish and French colonies of North America. He won the personal admiration of the Kings of France and Spain, took the city of Havana in Cuba back from the British at the end of the Seven Years War and commanded the Spanish expeditionary force that tried to take Algiers in 1775.

His fame was such that the poet Byron mentioned him in his epic satirical poem *Don Juan*; Byron has the great lover's wife, Donna Julia, talk of her spurned Irish lover, saying, 'Was it for this that General Count O'Reilly, who took Algiers, declared I used him vilely?' In his own footnotes on the canto that mentions the Meath man, Byron dryly notes that 'Donna Julia here made a mistake, Count O'Reilly did not take Algiers – but Algiers very nearly took him.' It is a reference to one of the famous Irish general's rare defeats.

O'Reilly had a long and lucky life, and was a fighter until the end. As a young man, he had a miraculous escape while seriously wounded on a battlefield in Italy, winning a last-minute reprieve from the *coup de grace* through the intercession of another Irishman, fighting on the opposing side.

And when the old soldier finally died at the age of seventy-two, it was while commanding a Spanish army charged with opposing French revolutionary forces invading Spain, shortly after the beheading of Louis XVI. He fought in the War of the Austrian Succession and the Seven Years War, governed Madrid and Cadiz and brought his iron rule to further-flung Spanish colonies and islands.

Through a decades-long career that stretched from battles in Prussia to sieges on Caribbean islands, O'Reilly showed uncommon military, diplomatic and political talents.

He was a success in love as well as war, and married one of the most beautiful young women of the Spanish-Cuban aristocracy, Doña Rosa de Las Casas, beginning a noble line on the island that only ended with the arrival of socialism under Fidel Castro.

To many in Spain, Cuba and Puerto Rico, Alexander or 'Alejandro' O'Reilly was a hero. There are still streets and squares named after the Irish soldier in Havana, New Orleans, San Juan, Puerto Rico, Barcelona and Cadiz (*Calle O'Reilly* in Havana's old town has a Café O'Reilly, which regularly hosts performances by Irish musicians visiting the Cuban capital). But he was also a cold-eyed executioner, called a 'monster and a despot' in his day and remembered for many years after his death as 'Bloody' O'Reilly, the soldier who brought the vengeance of a Spanish

Above: James 'Sligo' Jameson (1856-1888), scion of the whiskey distilling family, naturalist, artist, explorer and member of the Emin Pasha Relief Expedition, Africa, 1886-1889.

Above: The explorer Henry Morton Stanley (centre) with his officers (l-r) Dr Thomas Heazle Parke, Robert H. Nelson, William G. Stairs and Arthur Jephson.
Below: Irish military surgeon Dr Thomas Parke sucking poison from the side of Lieutenant Stairs during Sir Henry Morton Stanley's Emin Pasha Relief Expedition. Lieutenant Stairs had been hit by a poisoned arrow, which would probably have killed him, had it not been for Parke's prompt action to remove the toxin.

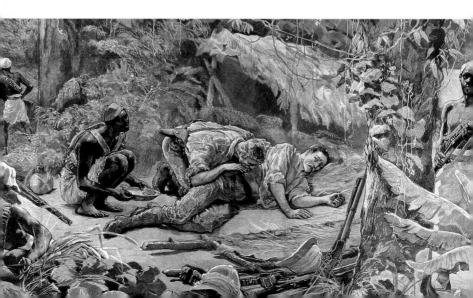

Right: The Walsh Family Coat of Arms featuring a swan pierced by an arrow – the motto translates as 'Transfixed – But Not Dead'.

Below: The Renaissance Château de Serrant in the Loire Valley bought by the Irish slaver Antoine Walsh in the mid-1700s – it remained in the Walsh family for almost a hundred years and is still in private ownership today, though open to the public.

Left: Dom Pedro I (1798-1834) Emperor of Brazil, who commissioned the Cotter Expedition.

Right: Hugh Gough. The Limerick-born General was one of the most successful and ruthless soldiers of the British Empire in the 19th Century. Gough commanded the forces that defeated the Chinese in the First Opium War.

Left: Alejandro O'Reilly: soldier, governor, Meathman, executioner.

Battle of Sobraon, Punjab, 10 February 1846: Limerick's Sir Hugh Gough defeats a much larger army of Sikhs in the last, bloody battle of the First Sikh War. Sir Hugh displayed his characteristic total disdain for his personal safety. The huge financial penalties imposed by the victorious British included the transfer of the fabulous Koh-i-noor diamond to the British Crown. Almost ten thousand Sikh soldiers were killed.

Left: William Burke, Irish-born serial killer who stalked the streets of Edinburgh.

WILLIAM BURKE.
as he appeared at the Bar.
taken in Court.

Right: Dr Robert Knox (1791-1862). The Scottish surgeon, anatomist and ethnologist is most famous for involvement with the body snatchers and murderers Burke and Hare.

Right: William Hare. He won immunity from prosecution by turning on his former partner in crime, William Burke (opposite page).

WILLIAM HARE.

as he appeared in the witness box, taken in Court.

Below: Thomas Francis Meagher (1823–1867), Union Army General during the American Civil War and admirer of Malachi Martin.

Left: Vincent Coll. With his trademark pearl fedora in the foreground, the Donegal-born killer strikes a relaxed pose as he unexpectedly wins bail on charges of child-killing.

Right: Vincent Coll and his defence lawyer Sam Leibowitz are all smiles after Judge Corrigan directs that he be freed on murder charges in one of the most controversial court cases of the Roaring Twenties.

king to New Orleans.

O'Reilly also had a macabre sense of theatre; for the French Creoles of Louisiana, who tried and failed to oppose Spanish rule, 'Bloody' O'Reilly was a man from whom you should never, ever accept a dinner invitation.

Alexander O'Reilly was born on his family's estate at Baltrasna, at Ashbourne in Co. Meath, in 1723 and baptised on 24 October of that year. His father was Thomas O'Reilly, who had married Rose MacDowell of Co. Roscommon; together they had four sons. The O'Reillys were a military family and the Baltrasna clan was a branch of the famous O'Reilly or 'Ó Raghallaigh' of Breffni (today, Co. Cavan), military chieftains who reached the height of their power in the fifteenth century.

One of Alexander's ancestors was the great Cavan folk hero Myles 'The Slasher' O'Reilly who — in legend at least — died defending the bridge of Finea in Co. Westmeath against English and Scottish forces under General Monroe in 1644 (The Slasher was undone by a sword thrust through his cheek, delivered by a 'giant Scotchman', according to an inscription on a Celtic Cross that marks the spot). The Slasher is said to have fallen at the bridge, but an alternative story from a contemporary source says he escaped by 'spurring his charger over the battlement and later went to France where he died'. Yet another history of The Slasher, which has gained some currency in recent years, has him missing the battle altogether and slipping away home to Cavan the night before, where he raised a large family and died happily, a relatively old man (or at least older than he would have been if he had stayed around to face giant, homicidal Scotchmen on the bridge at Finea).

Whether he fell, escaped to France or decided discretion was the better part of valour, an epic poem written long after the event by Ulster bard William Collins, gave The Slasher an appropriately heroic and melodramatic send off:

'But alas for the cause of Green Erin,
The heart of that hero is cold.
He died waving free in the blast,
With his hand on the hilt of a sword.'

After the demise or disappearance of The Slasher, Alexander's grandfather John O'Reilly kept up the family tradition by raising a regiment to fight for the Catholic King James at the Battle of the Boyne in 1690, shortly after which the family settled in Co. Meath. There is little doubt that the young Alexander, growing up in the ancestral home during unhappy and dangerous times for the defeated Catholic nobility, would have heard many tales of ancestral derring-do on the battlefields of Ireland. The boy would soon get his own chance to carry on the family business, far away from the fields of Co. Meath.

Sometime before his tenth birthday, his parents decided to leave the unpromising landscape in Ireland and relocate to Spain, with Alexander's, father, Thomas hoping to find service in the army of the Spanish king, as so many Irish nobles and freemen had done before him. They had little choice; the defeat of the Catholic nobility meant flight or subjugation.

The Irish in Spain were just one branch of The Wild Geese, the many thousands of Irish exiles who fought for the Catholic Kings of Europe, in France, Spain and Austria. It was the hard life of exiled, mercenary soldiers and on a number of occasions Irish regiments fighting under different flags had to face their own countrymen across a battlefield.

The O'Reillys relocated to Zaragoza, where Alexander, or 'Alejandro' as he was now called, showed a talent for adapting to the local language and customs that ensured a quick transition from Irish country boy to young Spanish gentleman. At the age of eleven, Alejandro O'Reilly enlisted in the Spanish service as a cadet, joining the Hibernia Regiment, one of six regiments of Irishmen fighting for the King of Spain; they were also known as 'O'Neill's Regiment', after the Old Irish noble family who had established themselves on the Iberian Peninsula following the Flight of the Earls.

Alejandro O'Reilly was a good young soldier, winning promotion to the rank of Sub Lieutenant in 1739, the year the War of the Austrian Succession broke out. It was a dynastic war, centred on the right of Maria Theresa to succeed to the House of Hapsburg, rulers of the Austrian Empire and it involved all the major European powers.

Spain was at war with Britain and Austria and the Hibernian

Regiment was sent to Italy to fight against the armies marching under the Double Headed Eagle of Austria. During the Battle of Campo Santo on 8 February 1743, Lieutenant O'Reilly, who had already been promoted for his bravery in the field, was shot and badly wounded, taking an Austrian musket ball to the thigh.

Aged just twenty-one, he lay on the battlefield through the night, surrounded by the dead, dying and wounded. The next morning, he was discovered by an Austrian soldier who was about to finish him off with a bayonet. Young Alejandro thought quickly and managed to convince the Austrian that he was from a wealthy Spanish family, the son of the Duke of Arcos, and that the Duke would pay a handsome bounty for his safe return. He was taken before the nearest Austrian officer, who turned out, as luck would have it, to be the Irish-Austrian Field Marshall, Maximilian Ulysses Browne.

Field Marshall Browne, who would later die in battle before the gates of Prague, was also a son of the Wild Geese. His father Ulysses Browne, one of the Brownes of Co. Limerick, had been forced to leave Ireland for service in Austria after the battle of the Boyne, where he would have fought alongside Alejandro's grand-father.

Browne saw through the young Irishman's flimsy ruse, even though Alejandro spoke fluent Spanish. It may have been that he could not have mistaken a young Meath man, one of his own countrymen, for a true-born son of the very highest of Span-ish nobility. However, as an account of O'Reilly's adventures in the *London Review* magazine of July 1777 records, Field Marshall Browne 'pleased with the deceit, ordered his physicians to attend him [O'Reilly] and sent him back with *éclat* to the Spanish camp'. The event had a romantic postscript. The Duchess of Arcos, when told about the young Irish officer who had escaped death by claiming to be her 'son', formed a life-long attachment with Alejandro and used her considerable influence to secure him rapid promotion.

The treaty that finally ended the war between Austria and Spain in 1748 ended years of turmoil in Europe, allowed Maria Theresa to remain on the Austrian Throne and normalised relations between Spain and Austria; it also allowed Alejandro the opportunity to serve with the Austrian army and become a keen student of the rapidly-changing science of military strategy and especially fortifications.

The skills that Alejandro learnt would later be put to great use, allowing him to build fortifications in Havana and Cadiz that still stand to this day; the fortress in Havana was once used as a HQ by Fidel Castro during his revolution, while the works in Cadiz are now a World Heritage Site.

The Prussians under Frederick the Great were revolutionising the way armies were organised and wars were fought. The new thinking became required reading for all ambitious military officers, no matter which flag they marched under.

The exchange of officers between armies, as military attachés or under similar terms, was very common at the time, even between nations that had recently been at war and O'Reilly was able to study these techniques for three years before returning home to Spain and to play a leading role in the modernisation of the military forces of King Charles III.

During his time in central Europe, moving between armies as an aide-de-camp, attaché or simply a young officer interested in the latest thinking, the dashing young Irishman came to the attention of the French king Louis XV, who was said to be very impressed with his talents.

Shortly after his return to Spain in 1762, O'Reilly was able to play an important role in a new war, this time with Portugal, winning advancement to the rank of Brigadier General by the age of forty.

Alejandro was now the rising star in the Spanish military establishment and was despatched to Havana, Cuba as the second-in-command to the new Spanish Governor of Cuba, the Count de los Ricla. The island's capital had been captured by the British during the most recent war, but was due to go back to the Spanish crown under the treaty of Aix-la-Chappelle.

O'Reilly landed in the harbour (the spot where he came ashore now has a street that bears his name) and watched as the last British transports and men-o-war sailed out of Havana. The young general was keen to put the latest in military thinking, learned under Frederick the Great's Prussian officers, to practical use in Cuba and set about completely rebuilding the harbour defences, which had miserably failed to stop the British several years previously.

Within a year, Alejandro had also met and married the beautiful Dona Rosa de Las Casas, the sister of the Governor of Cuba; their five children and their descendants would go on to play prominent roles in the history of Cuba, the US and Spain. Sadly, we know little of their private lives together, beyond the fact that Dona Rosa must have been a very patient woman as her Irish husband rarely stopped moving, planning or fighting.

In 1765, the energetic young general, by now a personal favourite of the Spanish king, Charles III, was on his way to Puerto Rico, another Spanish colony in need of reorganisation. Today, he is still remembered as the 'Father of the Puerto Rican Military' after his sweeping reforms of the island's forces and fortifications. He also showed a talent for civilian government, even if his arrogant ways seemed to ruffle feathers wherever he went.

With the common soldiers, his iron – and sometimes brutal – discipline, which included severe corporal punishment for slackers, caused some controversy, even amongst the Island grandees who were not usually concerned with the plight of the common private.

The Ministers in Madrid were delighted with his reforms and O'Reilly was made Inspector of Infantry and invested in Spain's highest chivalric order as a 'Knight of the Order of Alcantara' in 1765; for his part, O'Reilly recommended to the King of Spain that as many Irish immigrants as could be found be sent to Cuba to strengthen its military and economy.

It was back in Madrid in March 1766 that O'Reilly was able

to offer direct help to his admirer, King Charles; when serious civil unrest broke out, with rioting in the streets and attacks on Government ministers, a mob descended on the Royal palace and Charles III was in grave personal danger. O'Reilly, back from the Caribbean, moved quickly, assembling a small, scratch-force of soldiers and driving off a huge horde of outraged *Madrillinos* just as they were poised to break into the royal apartments. If he had reason to admire the young Irishman before, Charles could now credit him with saving his life and the lives of his family. Alejandro's reward was the command of a large Spanish force, which was about to be despatched to America.

Spain had gained possession of the old French colony of Louisiana through a secret clause in a treaty signed between the states six years earlier. The French colonists and Creoles (the people of New Orleans and the surrounding region who saw themselves as French) would not accept this sell-out. They revolted, declaring they would never accept the rule of the Spanish king. The first Spanish governor sent to Louisiana had been run out of town. With the British watching and her restive Caribbean colonies ready to act on any sign of weakness, Spain had to take decisive action.

The instructions from Charles III to O'Reilly were clear: 'Trusting in your ability and notorious zeal for my royal service, I have destined you to depart for America ... to take formal possession of Louisiana ... to organise legal proceedings and to chastise, conforming with the law, the exciters and associates of the insur-

rection ... you shall establish military as well as political adminis-
tration of justice. I entrust you with extensive and full power and
authority ... and if necessary to use force.'

Stopping first in Havana to add two thousand troops to his
large force, O'Reilly sailed into New Orleans in August 1769 with
twenty-four ships and an iron determination to impose the will of
the Spanish crown on the former French colony.

The dashing young Irish officer had become a strong-willed,
ruthless general. His contemporaries spoke of a taciturn, calculat-
ing solider, not given to much frivolity, with a brilliant organisa-
tional mind and a keen understanding of human weaknesses and
pressure points. The fearful population of New Orleans, knowing
full well the Spanish reputation of barbarity in the face of rebellion, would be treated to a brilliantly-effective, stage-managed
arrival. And then they would get the iron fist.

On that hot and humid August day, the massive Spanish fleet
sailed, ship by ship, into the harbour at New Orleans. The Louisiana port city at the time was an exotic polyglot place, with ships
bringing slaves, settlers and goods from across the Atlantic and
loading cargoes of cotton and other cash-crops for the return trip
to Europe. The people of New Orleans were used to running
their own city with the nominal overview of the French. They
would have dreaded the arrival of the Spanish, famous for their
autocratic, brutal rule. As O'Reilly's fleet dropped anchor, the harbour would have been crammed with commercial shipping. The
locals must have been stunned by the sudden appearance of so

large a Spanish fleet. Contemporary accounts speak of an eerie silence that hung over the wide harbour as the sun went down on a sweltering day and the menacing Spanish ships showed no signs of life or their intent.

O'Reilly wanted to build the tension. He waited until sunset before a single cannon was fired. Boats were lowered and column after column of Spanish troops, many of them Irishmen from O'Reilly's own Hibernia regiment, came ashore, with muskets presented and new uniforms glowing in the late evening sun. The large, well-drilled force lined three sides of the main square, which was laid out in the French style and bordered by pretty, American-colonial style town houses, stores and official buildings.

Still, there was no real sound from the Spanish ships or troops but the tramp of boots and the clash of arms being presented.

Then, at a signal, giant Spanish standards were unfurled and at the massed shout of '*Viva El Rey!*', the cannons of the Spanish fleet broke out in a series of shattering, rippling salutes. This was shock and awe, the General wanted the city to know that a new power was in place, one that they had no hope of resisting.

Finally, General Alejandro O'Reilly was announced to the populace and stepped ashore. A tall, thin, unsmiling figure, he was recognisable from the famous limp, a reminder of that battle in Italy some two decades previously.

The population were suitably cowed. They had already sent emissaries to O'Reilly, promising to end their rebellion and pleading for leniency, but they must have realised that their bold rejection of the Spanish King and his Governor would have consequences. What happened next would give rise to the legend of 'Bloody' O'Reilly.

When he had moved into the Governor's Palace, O'Reilly announced that there would be a grand reception for the most prominent people of New Orleans, as a sort of 'getting to know you', 'let-bygones be bygones' affair. The leaders of the rebellion, whom O'Reilly had already identified, were shocked to find themselves on the guest-list. This is not what they were expecting from the ruthless *generalissimo* sent by Madrid to crush their opposition to Spanish rule. They were even more surprised to find their new Governor the very soul of geniality, charm and hospitality on what was a glittering night in old New Orleans. The wine flowed and the tables were laden with the finest food. And when his guests were sated and a little fuddled with wine, O'Reilly's men moved in, bodily seizing six of the most prominent leaders of the rebellion and detaining scores more.

It had been a trap. The Creole leaders had stepped into a gilded cage and were dragged off to prison while O'Reilly prepared his next move.

The following morning, he announced that all citizens of Louisiana would swear an oath to the Spanish King. Only the ringleaders would face trial. But if anybody wanted to join them, there was plenty of room in the prison. After a series of trials, six prominent New Orleans men were sentenced to death. Many more were given long prison sentences. Their homes, their lands and businesses were forfeit to the Spanish crown. It was death for the ring-leaders, ruination for their followers and their families. One rebel leader died in prison. Five more were shot by firing squad on 25 October 1769. They had to be shot because no hangman could be found in Louisiana who was willing to do the job.

In that one calculated act of brutality, O'Reilly had quenched any desire for rebellion in the colony. And he had done it right out in the open for all to see. As he reported to the king, 'There is nothing that makes a government milder and more respected than to render to each misdeed the justice which is due it. I recommend this subject very particularly.'

The French government and popular opinion in Louisiana and beyond was outraged. The General was dubbed 'Bloody' O'Reilly, a name that lived on in infamy long after the Irishman had departed New Orleans.

However, in some ways, O'Reilly did a lot of good in New Orleans. He banned the practice of using 'Indians', as the indigenous population were called, as slaves and made it easier for black slaves to buy their freedom. He also reorganised the city, bringing in regulations and by-laws to cover everything from the operation of brothels and inns to butcher shops. Within a year, O'Reilly was on his way back to Madrid, leaving behind a strong colonial Governance and three very capable Irish officers, Arthur O'Neill, Charles Howard and Maurice O'Connor, who would go on to play significant roles in the development of Louisiana.

On his return to Court in 1770, Alejandro O'Neill was given the title 'Count O'Reilly' and made Governor of the City of Madrid.

He would face one major set-back in his career: an abortive attempt by the Spanish to take Algiers in 1775. The Spanish King wanted to hit back at the Sultan Mohammed III for his attack a year previously on a Spanish possession on the Moroccan Mediterranean coast. It was also an excuse for the expansion of Spanish territories into Algeria and to clear out the Barbary pirates who operated from the coast.

The massive amphibious operation, involving up to thirty-thousand troops, was a high-profile disaster for the commander, General O'Reilly.

While their gunboats became stuck in shallow waters, their forces landed in the wrong place and then walked straight into a carefully-laid trap. They were surrounded, subjected to withering artillery fire and driven back into the sea.

It was only Alejandro's beloved Hibernia Regiment, who staged a heroic rear-guard action against vastly superior forces, which prevented a total massacre. It was a humiliating defeat for the Spanish Crown, with two thousand soldiers lost and O'Reilly taking the blame for the debacle.

In the popular press, derision was heaped upon 'Bloody' O'Reilly, the general who had shamed Spain in New Orleans (hindsight is a wonderful thing for journalists) and had confirmed himself as a *mala suerte* or person who brings bad luck.

In a scurrilous street-ballad of the time, the 'foreign' General was ridiculed:

'*Oyendo de los moros el tiroteo, dijo O'Reilly temblando, '¡Ay, que me meo!*' ['Hearing the shots of the Moors said O'Reilly trembling, 'Oh, I've pissed myself!']

Lord Byron joined in the fun with more genteel verse.

These were tough times for the many Irishmen, the despised 'foreigners', who had advanced to significant posts in Madrid. Many of them had secured high office and influence at the expense of Spanish noblemen. Now their shining star, the King's favourite, had overseen one of the worst military disasters in decades. It was the chance that Alejandro's enemies at court, with little love for the upstart Irish, had been waiting for.

But while his reputation was damaged, O'Reilly could still count on the support of the king. After a brief banishment, he returned to his position as a grandee of the Empire, even if his imperious bearing was not to everybody's taste. The much-travelled English writer and soldier, Major William Dalrymple, met with O'Reilly in Madrid in 1774 and was not overly enamoured of the Irishman. In his *Travels Through Spain and Portugal*, he recalls,

'The governor of Madrid is the famous O'Reilly and the conduct of this general in New Orleans proves how perfect he is to execute the orders of a government of absolute power:

'When I went to see him, I found him especially arrogant and imperious. The powers at his disposal mean that he is surrounded by flatterers, but his despotic character makes him hated and despised by the people.'

It may have been a mutual loathing, O'Reilly was said to have found the Englishman to be a bit of a funny fish, especially after Dalrymple advised him, while they were strolling in his garden at night, to wear a hat against 'moonstroke'. We can only imagine how that went down with the old soldier.

O'Reilly had gone into retirement in Cadiz, his last port of call as a governor, when at the age of seventy-two, he was called upon to lead Spanish forces against the French revolutionary armies pouring over the Pyrenees in the Spring of 1794.

The old general was said to be enthused about his last command. But he never saw the French, dying suddenly in the small village of Bonete, near Albacete in Castilla-La-Mancha, South East Spain on 24 March 1794. He had been on his way from Cadiz to the battle-front, but died close to a small orange grove on the outskirts of the pretty village far from the border with France.

Shortly before his death, he had paid an 'Irish gentleman one thousand guineas to preserve his pedigree', to write down his personal history and the history of his family, ensuring that his own story would be written down for subsequent generations.

He was buried in Bonete, in the small village cemetery. Alexander O'Reilly was an exile of the Catholic gentry of Ireland, a soldier in a foreign army from the age of eleven, a brilliant military mind, a despot, hero, friend of kings and executioner. It was quite a life.

Interesting O'Reilly Connections

Alejandro O'Reilly's descendants in Cuba carried the title of Counts of Castillo and Marquis of San Felipe y Santiago.

One of his descendants, Robert Maitland O'Reilly (1845-1912) was surgeon general in the US Army from 1902 to 1909 and personal physician to US President Grover Cleveland.

Some believe the saying 'the life of Reilly' was inspired by the O'Reilly family's fifteenth-century practice of making their own coinage by 'clipping' English coins. At that time, a man who was flat broke, was said to 'not have a Reilly to his name'.

Another O'Reilly descendant, Frederick O'Connor, wrote about his childhood in the old house at Baltrasna in the eighteenth-century air, 'The Old House'. Sung to the air of the popular Welsh song, 'The Ash Grove', it was part of Count John McCormack's repertoire and was included in his farewell concert at the Royal Albert Hall.

As well as song-writing, Frederick kept up the family tradition, with a successful career in the British Army and a knighthood.

The Old House – Frederick O'Connor

Lonely I wander, through scenes of my childhood,
They bring back to memory those happy days of yore,
Gone are the old folk, the house stands deserted,
No light in the window, no welcome at the door.
Here's where the children played games on the heather,
Here's where they sailed wee boats on the burn,
Where are they now?
Some are dead, some have wandered,
No more to their home shall those children return.
Lone stands the house now, and lonely the moorland,
The children have scattered, the old folk are gone
Why stand I here, like a ghost and a shadow.
Tis time I was moving, 'tis time I passed on.

BEAUCHAMP BAGENAL
THE GENTLEMANLY ART OF LEGALISED MURDER

In an age when Irish duellists were the most feared in Europe, Beauchamp Bagenal earned a special notoriety for his short fuse and deadly skill with a pistol. A rake, a libertine, a 'true born Irish gentleman' skilled in the art of 'legalised murder', Bagenal could have strode straight from the pages of a bawdy Georgian play or rode out, spurs flashing, from the verses of a popular ballad. He drank, despoiled and whored his way across Europe, fought duels with an English Chief Secretary in the Phoenix Park and represented both Enniscorthy and Carlow in the Irish parliament as a staunch Nationalist and defender of Catholic rights.

In an era of romantic, larger than life figures, he was celebrated as the 'handsomest man in Ireland' and the greatest duellist of his age. Sir Jonah Barrington, the Laois-born lawyer and romantic chronicler of colourful Anglo–Irish society said of Bagenal: 'Amongst the people he was beloved, amongst the gentry he was popular, and amongst the aristocracy he was dreaded.'

The Bagenals first moved into Irish society with the marriage of Mabel Bagenal to Hugh O'Neill, Earl of Tyrone. Mabel was the youngest daughter of Sir Nicholas Bagenal, an English planter and soldier, and sister of Sir Henry Bagenal, Marshal of Queen Elizabeth's forces in Ireland. In the decades after the Elizabethan conquest, the Bagenals settled in the area of the river Barrow where they founded the town that would bear their name in later years: Bagenalstown, Co. Carlow. Beauchamp was born in 1735, the son of Walter Bagenal and Eleanor Beauchamp, and at the age of eleven inherited what had by this time become a huge estate. A drinker and a gambler from his teens, Beauchamp had already made a start on depleting the family fortune by the time he was due to finish his gentleman's education with the traditional Grand Tour of Europe. He even found it necessary to sell some land to fund two years of travel through the great cities of Europe, picking up expensive souvenirs and learning the manners of the courts of Europe where the wild and easily provoked Irish were often about as welcome as a dose of the pox.

It was during his Grand Tour that Beauchamp really started to build his reputation as the original Wild Irish Rover, as his biographer and great admirer Sir Jonah Barrington records:

'During his tour he had performed a variety of feats which were emblazoned in Ireland, and endeared him to his countrymen. He had fought a prince, jilted a princess, intoxicated the Doge of Venice, carried off a Duchess from Madrid, scaled the walls of a convent in Italy, narrowly escaped the inquisition at Lisbon, concluded his exploits by a duel in Paris; and returned to Ireland with a sovereign contempt for all continental men and manners, and an inveterate antipathy to all despotic Kings and arbitrary governments.'

The 'jilted princess' in question was Charlotte of Mecklenburg-Strelitz, afterwards married to Mad King George III of England. Charlotte was patroness of both Bach and Mozart and a close personal friend of Queen Marie Antoinette of France.

Duelling was beginning to go out of fashion in England and on the continent while Bagenal was a young man in Co. Carlow in the 1750s, but the Irish gentry still adhered to the more direct approach to settling disputes. So it was Beauchamp's good fortune, given his character, to be born into a society that positively encouraged well-bred homicidal maniacs to settle often petty disagreements via the business end of a flintlock pistol by Reads of Dublin or John Twigg of London; at least nineteen Dublin companies were making duelling pistols in the early nineteenth century and their guns were prized far afield. It was said that Irish gentlemen showed a 'singular passion ... for fighting each other' and one of the first questions asked of a potential son-in-law in Ireland was 'Did he blaze?'

The craze for settling disputes by mortal combat reached its peak in Ireland between 1780 and 1820. Historians who have looked at a sample of 306 duels fought in Ireland between 1771 and 1790 have found that there were sixty-five instant deaths and sixteen mortal wounds, but just under a third ended without injury. The Duelling Code or rules, which were laid out in an Irish court and recognised across Europe and America, allowed for honour to be served if, for instance, both men discharged their pistols without hitting the mark.

Almost all of the Irish gentry played the game. The great Irish politician Daniel O'Connell fought a famous duel at Bishop's Court Demesne, Co. Kildare on 1 February 1815, against a political opponent called John D'Esterre. O'Connell had previously been traduced as a coward by his political enemies for failing to follow through on a challenge he had issued to another lawyer two years previously. However, after D'Esterre, a noted duellist, took offence at a remark made by O'Connell during a speech made in January 1815 and challenged his honour, the Kerryman had little choice but to face his enemy on the field of honour. When they met on the agreed ground in Co. Kildare, both men fired at the same moment. D'Esterre missed, but O'Connell hit his opponent on the hip. It was first thought that D'Esterre had only suffered a light hit. But his seconds soon realised that he had sustained a mortal wound to the abdomen. He was carried to a nearby house where it took him two days to bleed to death. O'Connell was deeply shaken and displayed bitter remorse and regret to his dying day. It was said that, for the rest of his life, would wrap his right hand in a handkerchief when entering church, so as not to let the hand that had killed a man offend God. However, his bravery in facing his opponent down the barrel of a pistol undoubtedly enhanced the popular image of the politician who would go on to become The Liberator.

The gentry and the common people loved a duellist and it was expected of any man in public life to accept no slight, however small, on his character.

Not for nothing did the Irish aristocracy strive to have an 'heir and a spare', their sons were in severe and constant danger of meeting a premature death by pistol or sword.

On his return home from his Grand Tour of Europe, Beauchamp understandably decided that his unique skill-set was
most naturally suited to a career in politics. In the election of 1768, Bagenal and his running mate, William
Burton, made a simple appeal to the good voters of Carlow:
'To the gentlemen, clergy and freeholders of the county of
Carlow; Gentlemen, as the present Parliament will soon be
dissolved, we beg to offer ourselves as candidates for your
county, and request the favour of your votes and interest,
which shall be ever gratefully acknowledged by Gentlemen.'
Your most humble servants, Beauchamp Bagenal, William Burton.'

Beauchamp was duly elected to the Irish parliament in College
Green, an august institution that was at that time home to plenty
of colourful characters.

Finn's Leinster Journal of 20 July 1768 reported celebrations and
carousing on an epic scale: 'great celebrations and enjoyment on
the election of Beauchamp Bagenal and William Burton, Esquires'.

From 1768 until his retirement from public life in July 1783 he
continued to represent Carlow (with occasional interruptions) as
a member of Henry Grattan's party.

Bagenal was a Nationalist who always voted in favour of Catholic Relief Bills. He also moved the Bill that granted a large sum
to Grattan in recognition of his work leading to the legislative
independence of the Irish Parliament. To celebrate that independence, Bagenal held a review of Irish Volunteers close to his
ancestral home in Co. Carlow, which featured plenty of strong

drink laid on for all comers. The celebrations went on until the following morning, after which one observer recorded; 'the park was like a field of battle, strewed over with prostrate bodies.' Drinking with Bagenal was, like most of his other pursuits, competitive, deadly serious and potentially lethal. His home at Dunleckney hosted regular bacchanalian feasts that featured hard drinking and regular gunfire. Nicknamed 'King Bagenal' for his lavish entertaining, Beauchamp expected his guests to match him glass for glass and had a way of encouraging lightweights. Meals were 'primarily drinking bouts', according to one contemporary. And it was the unwise man who protested an early start in the morning. Jonah Barrington, obviously an admirer, noted; 'At table, he kept a brace of duelling pistols handy, one for tapping the barrel of claret, the other for dealing with any of his guests who failed to drink enough to send him reeling from the table.'

Irish history abounds in ironic footnotes and it is amusing, given Beauchamp's reputation as a drinker, that one branch of the family (the Mathews of Thomastown in Co. Kilkenny) would eventually produce Fr Mathew, founder of the Temperance Movement. But, while Beauchamp was a parliamentarian, squire of a large estate and the father of four, he never gave up on the true passion of his life and was 'out' (as the popular terminology of the time had it) on a regular basis. His favoured duelling spot locally was Killenane Cemetery on the main Kilkenny to Carlow road, on the outskirts of Bagenalstown. There, he would lean against a gravestone (he was lame in one leg from an early duelling injury), heft his pistol and casually invite his opponent to pick out a patch of ground suitable for his imminent interment. It was almost certainly in these sombre surroundings that one of his more notable duels occurred. His opponent on the field of honour was his godson (and later to be one of the executed leaders of the 1798 rebellion), Beauchamp Harvey Bagenal. Sir Jonah Barrington (who was a friend of Harvey's) records that Beauchamp Senior had apparently challenged his godson for no better reason than to find out if the youngster could live up to the family name.

'Harvey's reputed Kinsman provoked my friend to fight with him, in order to have the satisfaction of ascertaining, "whether or not the lad had metal [sic]" says Barrington. There may also have been a question of disputed paternity as Beauchamp apparently liked to boast of how he had sired half the children in the county – and, indeed, the estate was ultimately inherited by his natural daughter, Sarah Westropp.

The diarist continues:

'Mr Bagenal stood Harvey's fire, and immediately cried out to him. "You damned young villain! You had like to have killed your godfather – yes, you dog, or your own father, for anything I know to the contrary. I only wanted to try if you were brave. Go to Dunleckney and order breakfast. I shall be home directly."'

When he wasn't fighting his close relations (or demanding they get the black pudding on) Bagenal was also fond of taking the odd pot shot at authority. We know of a famous duel with the then Chief Secretary, a Colonel Blacquiere in 1773. The chosen ground was the popular 'thorn trees' in the Phoenix Park. Beauchamp was having a rare off-day and Blacquiere escaped injury, with the ball only getting close enough to take away some of his hair and the fur of his beaverskin hat. Age did not diminish the homicidal fire that burned in Beauchamp's belly, and even into his sixties he was still blazing away with gay abandon.

The Cork Nationalist MP, The O'Neill Daunt, recorded a duel fought between Bagenal and one of his neighbours, who had allowed his pigs to stray into one of the squire's flowerbeds. The pigs were sent back, *sans* tails and ears, and the challenge was issued. The elderly blade made only two requests from his opponent, firstly, due to his age and infirmity he wanted to fight sitting in an armchair and secondly, the duel should take place at a civilised hour as opposed to the traditional dawn. Beauchamp was uncharacteristically apologetic about his stipulations: 'Time was that I would have risen before daybreak to fight at sunrise, but we cannot do these things at sixty. Well, heaven's will be done.'

The outcome of this duel in the sun was that the unfortunate neighbour was badly wounded and Bagenal's chair was shattered. He himself was unhurt.

However, while contemporary diarists record a long career in gentlemanly mayhem, some historians believe that Beauchamp may have only fought a dozen or so formal duels. It seems that his legend may have been embroidered even as he lived, and simple tap-room skirmishes became bloody tales of murder and mayhem with the still twitching bodies of the landed gentry strewn left, right and centre. What is not, however, in dispute, is the fondness for duelling among his class, and, in fact, it was the Irish, in a rare burst of formality, who went so far as to draw up the rules governing the 'sport'.

The famous *Irish Code Duello* (set out in full below) was adopted at the Clonmel Assizes in the Summer of 1777, signed into law by Crow Ryan (President) & James Keogh & Amby Bodkin (Secretaries). The Code, more popularly known as *The 26 Commandments*, set out in great detail the means and manner by which proper judicial combat should take place. While the practice may sound barbaric to modern ears, the code was actually designed to ensure that honour could be satisfied with as little maiming or death as possible. For example, Rule 22 of the Duello stipulated: 'Any wound sufficient to agitate the nerves and necessarily make the hand shake, must end the business for that day.' Most duels ended without death or even serious injury. Interestingly, the code also included two extra rules specifically for Galway, a city where men were apparently prone to taking extra precautions if they could get away with it. These were:

1) No party can be allowed to bend his knee or cover his side with his left hand, but may present at any level from his hip to his eye.

2) None can either advance or retreat if the ground be measured. If no ground be measured, either party may advance at his

pleasure, even to touch muzzle; but neither can advance on his adversary after the fire, unless the adversary steps forward on him.

Galway gentlemen had traditionally held themselves apart, preferring to use the rapier or short sword long after the rest of the country (and especially the duelling hotbeds of the midlands and Dublin) had adopted the more progressive pistol. A well-made pistol was viewed at the time as the 'great equaliser', as becoming proficient in swordplay required long training and practice. 'Firearms,' one commentator noted, 'leave no inequality between combatants, but [that] of intrepidity.' To the good fortune of many duellists, pistols also turned out to be a safer bet when it came to survival. While a fifth of those involved in duels with swords died, just over one in twenty of those who fought with pistols perished as a result of their encounter (though a third were injured). The rules of the *Irish Code Duello* were accepted across Europe and in the United States as the gentlemanly way of settling a grievance. The most infamous duel in US history, involving Secretary of the Treasury Alexander Hamilton and Vice President Aaron Burr, was fought under the laws drawn up in Co. Carlow. Burr fought and mortally wounded Hamilton at Weehawken, New Jersey on 11 July 1804. Hamilton knew full well that his long time rival Burr was the much better sharpshooter. But because of the accepted codes of honour, he could not back down from Burr's challenge without opening himself up to public ridicule. Major Nathaniel Pendleton, one of Hamilton's friends, recited the accepted rules of duelling, as codified at the Carlow assizes, before firing commenced. Burr got off the first shot with one of the pair of Wogdon & Barton duelling pistols (the London-made pistols are today in the collection of bankers JP Morgan Chase & Co.) and Hamilton fell to the ground, suffering a mortal wound without getting off a shot.

In the US, duelling survived in the Southern states long after it had gone out of fashion in the Yankee north. In 1838, Governor John Lyde Wilson of South Carolina, wrote *Wilson's Code Duello,* the first official US adaptation of the *Irish Code Duello*. It formalized the US principles for settling a gentlemanly dispute. In the case of swordplay, the Code advised: 'the parties engage 'til one is well bloodied, disabled or disarmed; or until, after receiving a wound and blood being drawn, the aggressor begs pardon.'

But back to our hero, irascible and honour-bound to the end, Beauchamp Bagenal summed up his own philosophy on life in a letter to young male relatives that survives,

'In truth my young friends, it behoves a youth entering the world to make a character for himself. Respect will only be accorded to character. A young man must show his proofs. I am not a quarrelsome person – I never was – I hate your mere duellist; but experience of the world tells me that there are knotty points of which the only solution is the saw-handle. Rest upon your pistols my boys. Occasions will arise in which the use of them is absolutely indispensable to character. A man, I repeat, must show his proofs – in this world, courage will never be taken upon trust. I protest to heaven, my dear young friends, that I advise you exactly as I should advise my own son.'

Beauchamp Bagenal died on 1 May 1802, at the age of sixty-seven years, in his bed. They are not breeding his like any more. For which we should be very grateful indeed. While he struck terror into many who crossed his path, and, if the stories are true, not alone maimed but killed quite a few, history has, largely, forgotten him and those he fought. And those who did remember him, seemed to do so with admiration, if this description in the *Milesan Magazine* of June 1812 is anything to go by:

'Beauchamp Bagenal of the Co. Carlow was a man whose intellect was clear, whose education was perfected by the best masters and company, and whose fortune allowed him the full range of fancy that an Irishman will take at the expense of cash as well as of prudence.'

'Bagenal was the true born Irish gentleman. He was particularly gifted as to countenance and figure and was esteemed as men of fortune often are, but in his case with much truth the handsomest man in Ireland. He fought all before him and spent all he could muster and he never wanted a ready word, or like King Charles II "never said a silly thing and never did a wise one."'

★ ★ ★

The Irish Code Duello, as adopted by the Clonmel Assizes in the summer of 1777

1. The first offence requires the first apology, though the retort may have been more offensive than the insult. Example: A tells B he is impertinent etc. B retorts that he lies; yet A must take the first apology and then after one fire, B may explain away the retort by subsequent apology.

2. But if the parties would rather fight on, then after two shots each, but in no case before, B may explain first and A apologise afterwards.

3. If a doubt exists who gave the first offence, the decision rests with the seconds; if they can't agree, the matter must proceed to two shots or to a hit if the challenger requires it.

4. When the *lie direct* is the first offence, the aggressor must either beg pardon or fire until a severe hit be received by one party or the other.

5. As a blow is strictly prohibited under any circumstances amongst gentlemen, no verbal apology can be received for such an insult; the alternatives therefore are, the offender handing a cane to the injured party, to be used on his own back, at the same time begging pardon, firing on until one or both is disabled or exchanging three shots and then asking pardon without the proffer of the cane. If swords are used the parties engage 'til one is well bloodied, disabled or disarmed; or until, after receiving a wound and blood being drawn, the aggressor begs pardon. N.B. A disarm is considered the same as a disable; the disarmer may strictly break his adversary's sword; but

if it be the challenger who is disarmed, it is considered as ungenerous to do so. In case the challenged be disarmed and refuses to ask pardon or atone, he may not be killed as formality; but the challenger may lay his own sword on the aggressor's shoulder, the break the aggressor's sword and say, 'I spare your life!' The challenged can never revive the quarrel – the challenger may.

6. If A gives B the lie and B retorts by a blow, being the two greatest offences, no reconciliation can take place 'til after two discharges each, or a severe hit; after which B may beg A's pardon humbly for the blow and A may explain simply for the lie; because a blow is never allowable and the offence of the lie, therefore, merges into it. (See rule No. 5.) N.B. Challenges for undivulged causes may be reconciled on the ground, after one shot. An explanation or the slightest hit should be sufficient in such cases, because no personal offence transpired.

7. No apology can be received in any case after the parties have taken the ground, without exchanges of fires.

8. In the above case, no challenger is obliged to divulge his cause of challenge, if private, unless required by the challenged so to do before their meeting.

9. All imputations of cheating at play, races, etc. to be considered equivalent to a blow, but may be reconciled after one shot, on admitting their falsehood and begging pardon publicly.

10. Any insult to a lady under a gentleman's care or protection to be considered as, by one degree, a greater offence than if given to the gentleman personally and to be regulated accordingly.

11. Offences originating or accruing from the support of ladies' reputation to be considered as less unjustifiable than others of the

same class and as admitting of slighter apologies by the aggressor – this to be determined by the circumstances of the case, but always favourable to the lady.

12. In simple unpremeditated encounter the rule is – first draw, first sheathe; unless blood be drawn, then both sheathe and proceed to investigation.

13. No dumb shooting or firing in the air admissible in any case. The challenger ought not to have challenged without receiving offence; and the challenged ought, if he gave offence, to have made an apology before he came on the ground; therefore children's play must be dishonourable on one side or the other and is accordingly prohibited.

14. Seconds to be of equal rank in society of the principals they attend, in as much as a second may either choose or chance to become a principal and equality is indispensable.

15. Challenges are never to be delivered at night, unless the party to be challenged intends leaving the place of offence before morning; for it is desirable to leave all hot-headed proceedings.

16. The challenged has the right to choose his own weapon, unless the challenger gives his honour that he is no swordsman; after which, however, he cannot decline any second species of weapon proposed by the challenged.

17. The challenged chooses his ground; the challenger chooses his distance; the seconds fix the time and terms of firing.

18. The seconds load in presence of each other, unless they give their mutual honours they have charged smooth and single, which should be held sufficient.

19. Firing may be regulated – first by signal, secondly by word of

command; or thirdly, at pleasure, as may be agreeable to the parties. In the latter case, the parties may fire at their reasonable leisure, but *second presents and rests* are strictly prohibited.

20. In all cases a mis-fire is equivalent to a shot and a snap or a non-cock is to be considered a mis-fire.

21. Seconds are bound to attempt reconciliation before the meeting take place, or after sufficient firing or hits, as specified.

22. Any wound sufficient to agitate the nerves and necessarily make the hand shake, must end the business for that day.

23. If the cause of meeting be of such a nature that no apology or explanation can or will be received, the challenged takes his ground and calls on the challenger to proceed as he chooses; in such cases, firing at pleasure is the usual practice, but may be varied by agreement.

24. In slight cases, the second hands his principal but one pistol, but in gross cases, two, holding another case ready-charged in reserve.

25. Where seconds disagree and resolve to exchange shots themselves, it must be at the same time and at right angles with the principals, thus: - If with swords, side by side with five paces interval.

26. All matters and doubts not herein mentioned will be explained and cleared up by an application to the committee who meet alternately at Clonmel and Galway at the Assizes, for that purpose.

As mentioned in the main text, there were two further rules laid down for Galway: No party can be allowed to bend his knee or cover his side with his left hand, but may present at any level from his hip to his eye.

None can either advance or retreat if the ground be measured. If no ground be measured, either party may advance at his pleasure, even to touch muzzle; but neither can advance on his adversary after the fire, unless the adversary steps forward on him.

O'DWYER AND DYER
— THE BUTCHERS OF AMRITSAR

In April 1919, just three months after Eamon De Valera convened the first Irish parliament – the First Dáil – in Dublin, a Tipperary man and an adopted son of Cork were busy machine-gunning men, women and children in another part of the Empire.

Imperial Britain's worst single atrocity of the twentieth century was the direct result of the policy of violent repression formulated by a faithful Irish servant of the Raj and carried out by a soldier who was schooled in Cork and served as a young officer in Dublin and Belfast.

Sir Michael O'Dwyer and Brigadier-General Rex Dyer are largely forgotten now in Britain and Ireland, where the civil-servants and soldiers who brutally enforced imperial rule are at best an embarrassment. O'Dwyer, the son of a Tipperary landlord and the claimant of spurious, self-aggrandising connections to ancient Irish nobility, was of a class of Irish servants of the Empire who enthusiastically oppressed and exploited millions in far-flung possessions across the globe. Dispossessed and marginalised at home, these Irishmen found power, prestige and wealth in India and Africa, doing the dirty work of Empire and British commerce, extending the mercantile piracy of the East India Company or opening up China to the opium trade at the point of a bayonet.

O'Dwyer was unusual in that he ultimately did not escape his crimes. He was shot dead in London in 1940 by a vengeful assassin, a brother of a young Punjabi demonstrator killed by crown forces some two decades previously.

General Reginald 'Rex' Dyer, the Englishman who never really knew England, spending his childhood in India and his youth in Cork and Dublin, would die in his bed in England in 1927, with tributes following from the jingoistic sections of the British press who memorialised him as 'The Man Who Saved India'. The *Westminster Gazette* had a more realistic opinion, pointing to the crimes of the recently deceased Dyer and his political chief, O'Dwyer, and saying, 'No British action, during the whole course of our history in India, has struck a severer blow to Indian faith in British justice than the massacre at Amritsar.'

O'Dwyer and Dyer came from two very different lands, but from strangely similar worlds. Born in Solohead, Co. Tipperary, O'Dwyer had grown up as one of fourteen children of a Catholic landlord during the convulsions that rent the Irish countryside in the second half of the nineteenth century, when his father and the landowning class he belonged to faced death threats, arson attacks and the maiming of cattle. There was economic depression, the Land War and even famine after the failure of the potato crop for three harvests to the summer of 1879. In Ireland as a whole, there were some 2,590 'Fenian outrages' reported in 1880 alone. In O'Dwyer's home county of Tipperary, the outrages included the burning of crops and homes, the maiming or driving off of livestock, physical attacks on landowners and agents and threatening notices nailed to the doors of those deemed to be enemies of the common people. The constabulary had to set up check-points and offer round-the-clock protection to entire families threatened by the Fenians and land agitators.

As the Land War raged in Ireland, there was a flight of mainly Protestant gentry from the countryside. In 1885, for instance, an estimated one thousand Irish Protestant schoolboys were sent away to England by their worried families. Though he came from a Catholic family, O'Dwyer, too, was educated partly in England. As a child, he was educated by the Jesuits, forged a brilliant academic and sporting record at Balliol College at Oxford and entered the Indian Civil Service immediately after graduation. In 1912, at the age of fifty-four, he was made Lieutenant-Governor of the Punjab, and became one of the pillars of British rule in India.

Both Dyer and O'Dwyer had reason to fear the 'native mob', coming as they did from a 'besieged' ruling class. In the Indian hill stations of Dyer's childhood and in Ireland in the 1870s and 1880s, their homes and schools would have been as islands in a storm-tossed sea. Dyer was from an Anglo-English family that had been in the sub-continent since the days of Clive of India. The young Dyers would have grown up hearing terrible stories of the Indian Mutiny of 1857, when the Indian soldiers of the British army led a brutal insurrection against their masters, resulting in huge slaughter (mostly of Indians) and an enduring and almost primal paranoia amongst the white masters of the Raj. For their mother, who had witnessed the 'slaughter of innocents' during the mutiny, the British were always just a careless moment, one slip in discipline, away from yet another terrible conflagration. With both sides of the family of Anglo-Indian stock, they would have never known any life apart from the British Raj, with its relatively tiny military force and an always-precarious grip on power.

Dyer learnt Urdu as a child in the hill-station of Simla before being sent, with his older brother, Walter, (they were aged eight and ten) to school in Ireland; their father, who was involved in the brewing and distilling industry in northern India, may have heard of Middleton College from business contacts at the famous distillery in the North Cork town. When the two 'Wild Indians' arrived in Cork after a two-month journey from India (made alone) they were dressed in tropical suits and solar topi hats and each had a traditional Ghurkha knife, the fearsome *kukri*, tucked into a scarlet sash wrapped tightly around their waists. As if they were not different enough, Rex had a terrible stammer, which led to him getting into endless fist-fights with bullies. The future general only overcame his stammer by going for long walks in the Cork countryside, shouting sentences to himself at the top of his voice. Contemporaries later talked of Rex leading pitched battles against the local boys from the town, the 'Baminines' who would periodically invade the school playing pitches through gaps in the fence. The two sides fought 'Homeric battles with wickets, bats, fists, anything'.

O'Dwyer and Dyer, with more in common than they probably realised, would learn a lasting fear of uprising and revolt and dedicate their lives to imposing the rule of law, the absolute right of the Anglo-Saxon middle and upper classes to rule their 'inferiors'. However, what would link the two men directly was 13 April 1919 and Amritsar – 'The Massacre that Ended the Raj'.

Ever after, both would display the bitter, undying conviction, in the face of world opinion, that they were entirely justified in using Lee Enfield rifles, Vickers machine guns and Bristol fighter planes against unarmed civilians. Their aim, as O'Dwyer would proudly declare again and again after April 1919, was to teach the 'brown fellows' that 'revolution is a dangerous thing'.

Winston Churchill was the Imperial Secretary of War when the actions of Dyer and O'Dwyer were finally debated in the House of Commons, several months after the massacre. Churchill was no lily-livered liberal. In May 1919 he was advocating, in a secret memo to the War Office, the use of poison-gas bombs against 'uncivilised tribes' in modern day Iraq as part of a wider bombing campaign against Kurdish villages. Though the gas was never used, Churchill did order the RAF to carry out major bombing campaigns against civilian targets as part of his Mesopotamian 'war on the cheap' (in Churchill's words). The future war leader had crunched the numbers and decided that it was more cost-effective to flatten villages from the air than send in ground-troops. His orders to the RAF were to 'bomb any Kurds that look hostile'. But even Churchill, who would soon, as the crisis developed in India, call on the British authorities to let Gandhi 'starve to death', felt outrage at what happened at Amritsar, telling the House of Commons that the massacre was 'an episode without precedent or parallel in the modern history of British Empire ... an extraordinary event, a monstrous event, an event which stands in singular and sinister isolation.'

What happened in the Punjab on a mid-April day in 1919 is known to Western historians as 'The Amritsar Massacre' and to the Indians as the 'Jallianwala Bagh Massacre'.

The Raj was under growing pressure, dealing with calls for reform from liberals in England and increasing demands for autonomy from nationalist organisations lead by the Indian National Congress. The demands ranged from a kind of home rule for India to full and immediate independence.

In April 1919, Brigadier-General Richard Dyer, a fifty-five-year-old, highly-experienced soldier who had spent his formative years at Middleton College in Co. Cork and on the streets of sectarian-torn Belfast as a young officer, decided to make a point. Amid escalating tensions, rioting and the killing of several British citizens in the Punjab, Dyer, at the express instruction of O'Dwyer, had issued a series of orders that effectively put the region under marshal law and forbade the gathering of more than three 'natives' together.

On the morning of 13 April, thousands of civilians had gathered at the large, open Jallianwala Bagh compound to participate in the annual Baisakhi festival, a harvest celebration held to mark the start of the solar year and one with special significance for

Sikhs. The Bagh was a popular spot for festival-goers and pilgrims who would camp out in its broad open spaces overnight, wrapping themselves in blankets and lighting fires to cook their food.

Amritsar, nearby Lahore (today over the border in Pakistan) and the surrounding countryside were in a high state of tension following the attacks on British persons and property and the arrest and imprisonment without trial of local political leaders. Local Indian nationalists had planned to make political speeches in the Bagh, inviting the most respected citizens of Amritsar to read out letters sent from two political leaders from the area, Doctors Kitchlew and Satyapal, who had recently been arrested and imprisoned without trial by the British. A general strike would be proclaimed as part of the campaign to force the authorities to release the two detainees.

As plans were being made for the demonstration in Amritsar, Mahatma Gandhi, himself only recently released from British custody, was making a speech in Bombay in which he once again stressed the absolute importance of non-violent protest. He repeated his strong conviction that the political leaders arrested in the Punjab should submit to their imprisonment and there should be no mass demonstrations calling for their release.

Gandhi had actually been on his way to the Punjab, which was daily slipping into greater strife, when he was intercepted and detained, on the orders of Lieutenant-Governor Michael O'Dwyer, shortly before the Amritsar Massacre. Had O'Dwyer let the Mahatma reach the Punjab, he might have been able to calm the situation or at least make sure that there were no large political meetings to provoke the on-edge British.

The father of Indian nationhood was at the time only too aware of the potential for violence and for giving the British authorities an excuse to ratchet up their oppressive measures. In a long, open letter to his comrades in the Punjab, he had warned of the 'fundamental difference' between British civilisation and their own. 'They believe in the doctrine of violence or brute force as the final arbiter,' he had warned shortly before the massacre. However, given the increasing chaos and the slowness of communications, the Mahatma's warnings could not have reached the Punjab in time.

Despite all his warnings about potential violence, Gandhi, his followers in the Punjab and most of the thousands of peasants and political activists who had assembled close to the Golden Temple of Amritsar could never have anticipated what would happen next.

Most of the ordinary country folk gathering in the Bagh were probably unaware of General Dyer's declaration of martial law, which had been hastily proclaimed in the city even as they were pouring in from the surrounding countryside. They packed into the Bagh, a dusty, open space of almost seven acres bounded on all sides by mud-brick walls and accessible only through five entrances. As the Bagh filled up, the General and his troops arrived after spending the morning and afternoon shadowing a demonstration of over two thousand nationalists marching through Amritsar. The crowds were banging on empty kerosene cans and

chanting 'The British Raj is at an end!' and 'We will hold a meeting, let us be fired at.'

Four of the Bagh's entrances were only wide enough to admit
two or three people at a time. General Dyer ordered that the fifth,
wider, entrance be blockaded by soldiers and two armoured cars
carrying machine guns. Dyer had originally planned to take the
armoured cars inside the Bagh, but the entrances proved to be
too narrow for motor vehicles. As sunset approached, Dyer and
his soldiers, including a detachment of Ghurkha troops – recent
and raw recruits from Nepal – approached the narrow entrance
to the Bagh.

The General immediately ordered his fifty riflemen, made up
of a Sikh detachment and a section from the 59th Rifles Frontier
Force (which comprised 'native' troops and white subalterns and
officers) together with forty Ghurkhas, to enter the compound at
'the double'. Not all of the soldiers were armed with rifles; many
of the Ghurkhas carried only their fearsome *kukri* knives. They
were greeted by a vast crowd, with low estimates putting the numbers at fifteen thousand.

Within the Bagh, some were listening to speeches, some were
sleeping, others were cooking evening meals, and there was even
card playing and singing going on. Without warning, a large group
of soldiers rushed through the narrow passageway at one end of
the wide compound and began to spread out along a raised earth
platform in double file. A section of the crowd began to chant a
warning: '*Agaye, agaye*' ('They have come, they have come'), but

one of the speakers tried to reassure the crowd by shouting, 'Don't be afraid. Sit down. Government will never fire'.

There was no British order to disperse, no warning that shots were about to be fired. There were no warning shots. Dyer was not going to wait. He barked out the order: 'Ghurkhas, right! Fifty-ninth, left! Fire!'

The order was repeated by young British subalterns down the lines; a front rank of forty soldiers knelt, levelled their Lee Enfield rifles and fired a volley into the heart of the crowd.

The result was immediate and total panic. Bodies started falling and thousands of men, women and children scrambled in all directions to get out of the Bagh.

Witnesses later recalled how the soldiers continued a steady and accurate firing, as if they were on the practice range, mechanically pulling back the bolts of their rifles to eject spent .303 shells and carefully selecting their targets before shooting again.

The crowd were trapped inside the Bagh. Some tried to scramble over the walls; many of those who succeeded jumped to their deaths on the other side or were crushed by those coming after them. As the official enquiry later heard, the only movement Dyer made was to intervene to direct his riflemen to reload and fire 'upon places where the crowd was thickest'; Dyer pointed towards where people were trying to scale the walls or were massing at the narrow exits. Some who sought shelter behind a small shrine were picked off by the more accurate riflemen.

Several water buffalo were caught in the crossfire and went

down. Hundreds of people who escaped the actual bullets were crushed under corpses or trampled by the mob. In a small section of one narrow alleyway behind the Bagh there were a hundred and fifty bodies piled on top of each other like cord-wood. A walled well inside the compound provided some protection from the bullets, but not safety. A number of people who jumped into the open well in desperation were later found to have drowned. The firing went on for at least ten minutes. There were eerie silences when the ammunition ran out and the soldiers paused to reload.

The British Army had a term at the time that referred to the high rate of accurate fire that could be accomplished by a squad of trained riflemen. And the 59th Rifles were amongst the very best troops they could call on. The army called it the 'Mad Minute', estimating that a single soldier could aim and fire at least fifteen rounds at three hundred yards in sixty seconds. German soldiers who attacked trenches full of British riflemen during the First World War often mistakenly assumed they were facing multiple machine guns. However, with nobody shooting back and the target a mass of panicking civilians, there was no need for careful aim. Some soldiers could have fired up to twenty-five or more .303 rounds in a minute. One of the British subalterns later told the official enquiry, with some pride, that 'none of the men had hesitated or fired deliberately high'. The young officer was at pains to make this point after another witness had claimed that Dyer had intervened after some of the Ghurkhas had aimed high, shouting, 'Why are you firing high? Fire low. For what else have you been brought here?'

After almost ten minutes of non-stop rifle-fire, with hundreds of bodies scattered across the Bagh and hundreds more choking the laneways and drainage ditches surrounding it, Dyer ordered his soldiers to cease firing. It was a small mercy for the native people that Dyer had been unable to get his two armoured cars, carrying machine guns, into the Bagh. It was later suggested by Indian witnesses at the enquiry that he ordered the ceasefire, not out of any desire to spare further bloodshed, but because the soldiers had almost expended their total ammunition allowance and the General wanted to have some in reserve for the march back to base at the Ram Bagh.

Immediately after the shooting, the Ghurkhas who had been part of the firing were ordered to stand up, shoulder their rifles and unsheathe their kukris. They were ordered to advance in line towards the survivors. Several witnesses later said they were convinced the hillmen from Nepal were going to finish off the wounded. But after advancing a few yards, they were ordered to halt and rejoin the lines of soldiers who were now being reformed and turned back towards the exit.

Dyer strode briskly out of the Bagh to his waiting staff car without a glance back at the carnage. He is said to have remarked to a subaltern that he was glad that many had escaped, as they would carry the warning of British retribution to surrounding towns and villages. Behind him, over a thousand men, women and children lay dead, dying or wounded on the dusty ground of the Bagh.

Casualty estimates vary; the official British report later found that 379 people had been killed and over a thousand wounded. The Indian National Congress estimated that over a thousand had been killed and a further thousand or so wounded.

Amritsar was quiet that night for the first time in months as the local population and their political leaders tried to come to terms with the events inside the Bagh. The news was soon making its way to Government House in Lahore where Michael O'Dwyer, Lieutenant Governor of the Punjab, was in charge. O'Dwyer was described by contemporaries as a 'pugnacious, outspoken Irishman', known for his short temper, savage wit and implacable opposition to any sort of concessions to the people of India or their leaders; he is said to have had a fatherly affection for the ordinary Indian peasant, but deeply resented educated 'natives' like Gandhi, whom he accused of stirring up trouble for the Anglo-Saxons who had been ordained by God to guide and rule.

O'Dwyer was at Government House in Lahore in the hours after the massacre when the first, confused, reports started arriving from Amritsar shortly before midnight. A civil servant called Mr Jacob and an English school principal from the city rushed to Lahore by motorbike to deliver a personal despatch from Miles Irving, the Deputy Commissioner in Amritsar. The message stated: 'The Military found a large meeting of some five thousand men and opened fire without warning, killing about two hundred. Firing went on for ten minutes. I much regret I was not present.'

O'Dwyer's first concern was at reports (which turned out to be false) that English soldiers had done the firing; he had expressly told General Dyer to use 'native' troops where possible. It transpired that Dyer had followed this direction – the white officers had given the orders to fire and left the shooting to the 'natives'.

The Tipperary-man sent a brief report by telegraph to the Government of India informing them that General Dyer had issued a proclamation banning all public meetings, this proclamation had been ignored and a military action had occurred that had resulted in the deaths of around two hundred. As the full scale of the massacre quickly became apparent, other, more dramatic despatches were soon being sent by O'Dwyer, claiming that British officers had been attacked and killed and 'open rebellion' involving 'bands of marauding rebels' was now threatening the Punjab.

The following day General Dyer sent his first military report to his commanding officer and O'Dwyer, setting out the series of events as he saw it and saying, 'I realised that my force was small and to hesitate might induce attack. I immediately opened fire and dispersed the mob. I estimated that between two hundred and three hundred of the crowd were killed. My party fired 1,650 rounds'.

His commanding officer, General Sir William Beynon, and Sir Michael O'Dwyer then agreed on a response to be sent back immediately by aeroplane: 'Your action correct and Lieutenant-Governor approves'.

It was this brief dispatch, more than any other statement or action, which would cause O'Dwyer the most problems when the official enquiry eventually got underway. However, even as he was preparing the first reports for London, there was still mopping up to be done in the Punjab. Within forty-eight hours of the massacre, protests broke out in the town of Gujranwala.

On the instructions of the government men and the military commanders, police and aircraft were used against the demonstrators, resulting in twelve deaths and twenty-seven injuries. The officer commanding the Royal Air Force in India, Brigadier General NDK MacEwen later stated, 'I think we can fairly claim to have been of great use in the late riots, particularly at Gujranwala, where the crowd when looking at its nastiest was absolutely dispersed by a machine using bombs and Lewis guns.'

Most modern researchers, both British and Indian, now accept that the policy of teaching the Punjabi people a lesson that they would never forget was formulated by O'Dwyer, together with his bureaucrats and high-ranking military officers. There had been a secret, unofficial meeting at Government House in Lahore in the run up to the massacre where O'Dwyer, his top bureaucrats and his military men had decided on using 'native' troops to strike terror into the native population. The Indian troops serving the British, a mix of Sikhs, Muslims and Hindus from many different regions, were typically used for the dirty work.

In his self-serving account of his time in India, a book published in 1925 titled, *India As I Knew It,* O'Dwyer was unapologetic, remarking, 'The Punjabis were quick to take to heart the lessons that revolution is a dangerous thing.'

The months after the massacre at the Bagh brought condemnation from around the world and forced the British imperial government to set up an official enquiry, the Hunter Committee, which began its deliberations in Lahore in early November 1919.

General Dyer, in his evidence, was unapologetic, holding the line that he had no choice but to fire on the crowd. It was a matter of enforcing the rule of law and commanding the respect of the natives. When asked if he had done anything to help the wounded, he replied, 'No, certainly not, it was not my job. But the hospitals were open and the medical officers were there. The wounded only had to apply for help'. Dyer went on to claim that many 'ordinary Indians' had thanked him, after the massacre, for 'saving the Punjab'.

The Hunter Committee sat over a six-week period in Lahore. Sir Michael O'Dwyer wrote to the Viceroy of India to offer to give evidence. In a jarringly cheery tone, he wrote, 'I helped to set the military machine in motion and when the soldiers have been called upon to justify their actions it would not look well if the Arch-fiend stood aside.' When he eventually did give evidence, like Dyer, O'Dwyer stood firmly behind his policy of teaching the natives a lesson and refused to apologise, temporise or even explain. O'Dwyer claimed to have been informed, before the massacre, of an Indian plot to rise up and murder every Britisher in their beds. But he admitted he could offer no evidence.

In the end, the commission of enquiry declined to condemn Dyer, saying he had acted on the orders of his military and political superiors and carried out what were, in effect, orders. Sir Michael O'Dwyer was given what amounted to a mild rebuke.

General Dyer was, however, finished in India, relieved of his command, he returned home to a hero's welcome in England as 'The Man Who Saved India'. O'Dwyer was also no longer needed by the British in the Punjab, he would go into retirement to write a history of the O'Dwyer clan in Tipperary and become a regular on the lecture circuit, pugnaciously defending the right of the British people to rule over the darker-skinned peoples of the world.

It was during a speaking engagement for the conservative Royal Central Asian Society at Caxton Hall in London on 13 March 1940 that his actions in India finally caught up with him. Just as he finished an impromptu, fifteen-minute speech, during which, as *Time* magazine reported 'he turned his sarcastic Irish wit on the Indian nationalists, whom he still despised', he was shot dead by a Punjabi, Shaheed Udham Singh, who was acting in revenge for a brother killed at the Amritsar Massacre. Singh had himself been present at the massacre, part of a group of young boys from a local school who had been delegated to bring water to those gathered for the holy festival.

At Caxton Hall, Singh walked towards the podium and fired five shots from a revolver, which he had smuggled into Britain inside a hollowed out book, into O'Dwyer.

Singh, who was tried and executed for the murder, said at his trial,

'I did it because I had a grudge against him. He deserved it. He was the real culprit. He wanted to crush the spirit of my people, so I have crushed him. For full twenty-one years, I have been trying to wreak vengeance. I am happy that I have done the job. I am not scared of death. I am dying for my country. I have seen my people starving in India under the British rule. I have protested against this, it was my duty. What greater honour could be bestowed on me than death for the sake of my motherland?'

On 1 April 1940, Udham Singh was formally charged with the murder of Sir Michael O'Dwyer. He was committed to trial on 4 June 1940 at the Central Criminal Court, the Old Bailey, before Justice Atkinson, who sentenced him to death.

An appeal was filed on his behalf which was dismissed on 15 July 1940. On 31 July Udham Singh was hanged in Pentonville Prison in London. During the trial, Singh had made a request that his ashes be sent back to his country. His request was denied. However in 1975 the Government of India, at the urging of the Punjab regional Government, finally succeeded in bringing his ashes home. Thousands of people gathered at his formal interment to honour his memory.

* * *

There is a curious footnote to the story of O'Dwyer, Dyer and the Amritsar massacre.

In 1997, Prince Philip, the Duke of Edinburgh and Queen Elizabeth II were making what was already a controversial official visit to the memorial that now stands in the Jallianwala Bagh. Indian sentiment was divided on whether the British Royals should even have been allowed to enter such a sacred and blood-soaked site.

The Prince was shown the plaque that says: 'This place is saturated with the blood of about two thousand Hindus, Sikhs and Muslims who were martyred in a non-violent struggle.'

In an off-hand remark that provoked outrage in India, Prince Phillip observed: 'That's a bit exaggerated, it must include the wounded'. Few could have expected Prince Philip to quibble over the numbers at the very site of the massacre. The fact that he followed up this remark with a casual claim to a bit of second-hand information caused further offence; when asked by his shocked hosts how he worked that one out, Prince Philip nonchalantly explained: 'I was told about the killings by General Dyer's son. I met him while I was in the Navy.'

Somewhere, the ghost of Sir Michael O'Dwyer must have been saying 'Good show!'

MALACHI MARTIN
GODFATHER OF THE AMERICAN
CHAIN–GANG

Malachi Martin left Ireland in the mid–nineteenth century to escape the misery and death of the Famine years and to build a new life in America. He found wealth and political power, but only by inflicting misery and death on thousands in his new country.

Martin won honour in the Union Army of the Civil War, but then became one of the most reviled 'carpetbaggers' of the 'Reconstruction and Redemption' post-war period, when large areas of the South were effectively under military occupation and opportunistic Northerners could rise quickly. With whole regions of the former Confederacy in ruins, economically devastated and effectively lawless, the carpetbaggers were the infamous 'Yankee vultures' swooping in to feed off the carcass of the South. They bought up plantations at fire-sale prices, exploited the newly-freed slaves and secured political positions, patronage and power through the Republican Party. Eventually, Martin rose to become a boss-man in the most brutal, corrupt and dehumanising prison system ever seen in North America, where he cynically exploited the chain gang system to create an army of virtual slaves for exploitation by big business. The man who had left his own broken country for better things built his personal fortune on the back of convict labour. Ironically, he was also the inspiration for one of the first great campaigns towards penal reform in the US, following the *exposé* of the gulag system he helped build in Florida in a landmark book written by a former prison guard who witnessed the horror at first hand.

The Irishman became notorious across America for forcing convicts to work on his own lands or hiring them out as human beasts of burden to be worked to death. Thousands of prisoners were trapped for decades in a brutal penal system that could have them chained to the floor, locked in sweat-boxes, whipped, starved and left to die from disease. While Martin was not the only man to grow rich on the ruins of the South, he became a symbol of the decades-long exploitation of human misery on an industrial scale.

As with many Irish emigrants to the United States in the famine era, Malachi Martin was anxious to put the extreme poverty and hopelessness of his native land as far behind him as possible. He was born around 1822, probably in the west of Ireland where the Martins were concentrated around Galway and Mayo; in all official military and political records and census forms, his place of birth is simply put down as 'Ireland'. Martin arrived in New York harbour on the frigate *Gondola* on 11 August 1847, one of 113 steerage passengers embarked from Dublin. He was recorded as being a farmer of twenty-one years of age, with his native country given as 'Great Britain' (at that time, all Irish people would have been considered subjects of Great Britain).

'Black 47', as the year 1847 became known, was a terrible year in Irish history, remembered as the very worst summer of the Great Irish Famine. Successive summers of failure of the vital potato crop had led to famine, disease and a mass exodus of desperate men, women and children. A vast armada of ships, known as 'Coffin Ships' or 'The Fever Fleet' took hundreds of thousands of Irish refugees across the Atlantic. Most were cargo ships (including those that took grain and timber from Canada to Great Britain), returning westwards with human ballast in their cramped, dank and fever-ridden holds.

In 1847 alone, some 441 ships landed in Quebec, bringing eighty thousand of the estimated one hundred thousand Irish who fled to British North America in that year. Estimates vary, but it is thought that around one in ten of them would have died at sea or shortly after landing. Some 196,224 Irish people emigrated to the United States in 1847 alone (by the end of 1854, nearly two million people – about a quarter of the total population of Ireland – had emigrated to the US over the preceding decade).

Malachi Martin was just one of the many thousands fleeing the worst summer of the Great Famine. At twenty-one, he would already have seen his fill of human misery, either in the charnel house of the Irish countryside, the crowded, fever-ridden docks of Dublin or the hell of a six-week crossing in a coffin ship. But despite the hardship onboard the ships, the people were desperate to leave and willing to face the terrible crossing for the promise of a new life for themselves and their families; Martin's youngest fellow passenger on board the *Gondola* in New York harbour,

August 1847 was a four-month-old girl, Anne M. Beegan, who was travelling with her mother, three sisters and a brother, all aged under ten years.

Malachi Martin did build a new life for himself in the US, establishing a successful dry goods retail business in New York by 1852, some five years after stepping off the *Gondola*. His Irish-born wife (there are no records of her name) bore him a son called Walter in 1852 and is believed to have died shortly afterwards. His story was that of a typical immigrant-made-good and Martin might have stayed a small businessman in New York if it wasn't for the outbreak of the Civil War, or War Between the States, in April 1861.

At the age of thirty-eight, on 25 February 1862, Martin enlisted in the Union Army at the rank of second lieutenant and was commissioned an officer in the New York 15th Light Artillery Battery. He was old for a recruit, but there are signs that his business was not doing well and the pay and opportunities of life as an officer may have appealed to him, especially if he could use his dry-goods experience to find a post behind the lines and away from the fighting.

He was transferred to the US Volunteers Quartermaster's Dept, Infantry Regiment on 1 May 1862.

Martin served under Brigadier General Thomas Meagher, commander of the legendary Irish Brigade of the Army of the Potomac, which fought some of the fiercest battles of the Civil War, including the Seven Days' campaign, Antietam, Fredericksburg and Chancellorsville. The Waterford-born general mentioned his

Quartermaster in despatches from the Seven Days Battles, a series of six major engagements fought over seven days at the end of June 1862 near Richmond, Virginia. It was during this terrible week that Meagher and the Irish Brigade established their formidable reputation, standing firm and stopping a full-scale rout of Union forces as General Robert E. Lee's Army of Northern Virginia broke through the Federal lines at Gaines' Mills, before fighting a brave rearguard action that bought precious time for General McClellan's retreating Army of the Potomac.

When the dust had settled, Meagher found time to commend his officers and men, including 'Capt. Malachi Martin, the assistant quartermaster of the brigade, who with the heartiest alacrity volunteered his services on the occasion and fearlessly rendered me the most valuable assistance.'

After the battle of Fredericksburg in December 1862, Meagher again mentioned his Brigade quartermaster in his official report, closing his letter to his commanding officer by saying; 'In enumerating the members of my staff, I cannot omit Capt. Malachi Martin, the able and indefatigable quartermaster of the brigade, who has on several occasions stood the enemy's fire with me, and rendered at every risk important services to me in gallant style'.

By the time of Fredericksburg, Martin and the Irish Brigade had already been through the Battle of Antitam, the so-called 'Deadliest Day', the single most bloody one-day battle fought in American history.

Some twenty-three thousand soldiers were listed as killed, missing or wounded after twelve hours of almost unimaginable slaughter and heroism in the fields outside the village of Sharpsburg, Maryland on 17 September 1862.

At the height of the battle, the Irish Brigade was sent to charge across an open field towards a heavily-defended sunken roadbed that became known as 'Bloody Lane'. Of three New York Irish regiments numbering just over a thousand men, 512 were killed.

Meagher, his aides and the Brigade Chaplains led the way as hundreds of Irishmen stormed through withering fire at Bloody Lane (eight men who carried the green banner of the 69th New York were shot dead from under it). There were also Irish fighting and dying in Confederate grey on that day. The mostly Irish 6th Louisiana reported 50 per cent casualties, including the Irish-born Colonel Henry Strong.

Malachi Martin, who as a young man had escaped the famine, survived the bloodiest day of the American Civil War and the wholesale slaughter of his fellow countrymen. The Irish Brigade had been torn to pieces, but the remnants would fight on.

Martin went all the way south with the Union Army, serving in New Orleans and other parts of the South before ending up as quartermaster clerk in Tallahassee, Florida during the occupation by the Union Army.

On 20 May 1865, Union General Edward M. McCook of the occupying Union Army read President Lincoln's Emancipation Proclamation from the steps of The Knott House, on East Park Avenue in Tallahassee, officially marking the end of slavery for the black slaves of the town and across the South.

The Civil War was over. But for the conquered Confederacy, the era of the carpetbagger was about to begin.

The men who flooded into the vacuum left in the smashed South, with no slaves to work the plantations, dead or bankrupted owners and a general air of lawlessness and defeat, included former Union soldiers, businessmen, speculators, con artists, land-grabbers and well-meaning reformers who wanted to erase the memory of slavery and the bitterness of the war just ended. President Lincoln had promised an era of reform and redemption for the former rebel states. What actually happened was not so high-minded or clear cut.

In 1868, an editorial in a Pensacola, Florida newspaper summed up the widespread attitude towards the 'carpetbaggers' – named for the sturdy travel bags they carried, made from used carpet – amongst Southerners.

'While crushed beneath a grinding military despotism, hireling spies and impudent adventurers have swarmed upon ... [us] taking a despicable advantage of ... [our] weakness, misfortunes and suffering to traduce, vilify and malign ... [us] ... Upstarts, without name, character or position in their own land, have, with the aid of military power, imposed upon ... [the South] an odious government, and foisted themselves into office and power as ... rulers.'

The carpetbaggers were backed by the military occupation forces, granted loosely-defined powers to appropriate or buy (at punitively low prices) farmland and businesses; they generally acted like the agents of a conquering power.

Most of these 'upstarts' faded into history or were simply gentrified and absorbed into the life of the South by the passage of time. A few, however, are still remembered. And one of those is Malachi Martin, whose association with Florida's notorious 'Convict Lease' system assured him lasting infamy in the Deep South as a brutal and corrupt man.

With no real ties to the North and an eye for the great opportunities now open to former Union officers in the South, Martin was ideally positioned to make use of his business experience and his contacts within the new power system

After failing in two agricultural projects, both former slave plantations sold off for a pittance by their bankrupt and disenfranchised white owners, Martin moved into local politics with the Republican Party. Then from 1868 to 1877, the Irish-born soldier-turned-civil servant served as chief administrator and warden of the state penal institution at Chattahoochee.

While Martin was not the originator of the convict-lease system and could have claimed to have left the prison system before it become entirely pervasive, his reputation was sealed by the publication of a landmark account of the southern prison system, written by one of his former prison guards.

The writer, JC Powell, in his book *American Siberia: Or Fourteen Years In A Southern Convict Camp* (Chicago 1891), fostered the image of Martin as the archetypal evil prison warden and chain-gang boss. To Americans of the late nineteenth century, Siberia was a far off land of Tsarist prison camps and despotic inhumanity. They were shocked and outraged to learn that they had a Siberia of their own, located in the still desolate and lawless Deep South.

Powell, who had been captain of a convict labour camp in the Florida penal system, painted a picture of Malachi Martin as a carpetbagger whose regime was 'one of almost unrelieved barbarity.'

In *American Siberia,* Powell told the world that 'a man named Martin was warden [of the Chattahoochee prison], and the place was horror's den. He had been placed in charge of the building during the war, at a time when it was used as an arsenal. The state got rid of its criminals by turning them over bodily to him, and paid him bonuses amounting to over $30,000 for accepting the charge. He had vast vineyards and worked the convicts in them, manufacturing all kinds of wine, at which he made a fortune. There were no restrictions whatever placed upon him by the state.'

Powell was playing a little fast and loose with some of the facts. The former military arsenal at Chattahoochee had become a penitentiary immediately after the war, but Martin had come along some time after that. And while Martin was no doubt part of a brutal, corrupt and inhuman prison system (even by the standards of the time), he appears to have been spectacularly inept when it came to making his own personal fortune.

After his failed attempts at running two former plantations around the Tallahassee region, Martin worked his way into Federal Government positions (former Union Army men almost always got their rewards), serving as an agent of the Bureau of Refugees, Freedmen and Abandoned Lands from May, 1868. Part of his duties involved disposing of former rebel-owned plantations and helping their ex-slaves make the transition to freedmen. Martin failed to thrive in his government job and was almost bankrupt by November 1868, when his political connections landed him the job of the first commanding officer of the newly-created Chattahoochee State Penitentiary.

Even before the war, the Florida prison system had been, at best, disorganised and ad hoc, now the Federal Government and the newly reconstituted Florida Assembly wanted to take control. The old US Army arsenal at Chattahoochee, with its twelve-foot high, stone walls, was one of the few buildings capable of securely holding a large number of men.

There were problems, the citizens of Florida, already facing high taxes imposed to rebuild the state, did not want their tax dollars going towards an expensive prison system, so the state hit on an old-fashioned custom that would make the prisoners pay for themselves – convict leasing.

The Senate and Assembly of Florida voted in an act which would allow convicted criminals to be 'employed at hard labour' with the money generated going towards the running of the prison system. This would allow the prison governors to hire out convicts as labourers. It was seen as a way of punishing the prisoner while reforming him through hard work, and generating some much needed revenue into the bargain. The convicts were leased, body and soul, to contractors who would sublease to entrepreneurs in the agricultural, lumber or naval stores business.

In theory, the contractors were responsible for feeding, clothing and providing security for the leased prisoners. But in Florida and elsewhere, a system of 'discipline' left over from the just departed days of slavery on the plantations, led to terrible brutality and abuse. In the defeated South, still in turmoil and with lynchings, race-riots and paramilitary groups like the Ku Klux Klan terrorising former slaves and 'traitors', few lawmen or politicians were prepared to stand up for the rights of convicts. The system was wide open to abuse. In many cases, freed slaves, rootless and jobless, could be arrested and charged with 'vagrancy'. If they could not afford to pay the fine imposed on them by the county, they would be leased out to middlemen who could put them to work and cover the county fine.

Critics of the Convict Leasing system said it was simply the continuation of slavery, with the backing of the law. Florida and the rest of the south were desperate for cheap labour. Just before the war, fifty per cent of the population of Florida had been slaves. The white elite needed to find a way to get them back to work at the lowest rate possible (even better if they did not have to be paid at all).

In fact, former slaves caught up in the convict leasing system were actually worse off than they had been under slavery. Those who put the convicts to work didn't even bother to spend enough to ensure they were healthy, as they would have when they owned valuable slaves. As one former plantation owner, speaking after the war, put it,

'Before the war, we owned the negroes and if a man had a good negro, he could afford to take care of him. But these convicts, we don't own 'em. One dies, get another.'

The convicts were housed in ramshackle prison camps, often in desolate wilderness areas or on the edges of malarial swamps. Brutal working conditions meant they had a short life expectancy. They worked in phosphate mines, on turpentine plantations and on building roads and railroads (that made huge fortunes for Northern speculators). Prisoners could be flogged for the smallest transgressions. Those who tried to escape (and many did) would face terrible retribution when caught, severe floggings and the extension of sentences to the point were they were certain to be worked to death. Work gangs were chained together or to large iron balls which they had to drag every step of the way. And they were given just enough food and clothing to survive in the torrid Florida climate.

In *American Siberia*, Powell recounts the stories of convicts who inflicted grave injuries on themselves, including a man who gouged his own eyes out, in a bid to escape from the prison farms and road gangs.

Malachi Martin, as commandant of the state prison, would be paid five dollars a day plus bed and board, good pay and conditions in the economically depressed South of that time. And his position would allow him to greatly augment his income as long as he was prepared to bend the rules, or make up his own as he went along. That the system he worked in, which effectively gave warders, businessmen and middle-men control over a large, unpaid and literally captive workforce, might be open to abuse did not seem to trouble the politicians. At the end of 1868, Martin moved into the Chattahoochee Prison and got down to business.

The Irish-born prison boss was soon writing reports to his political bosses about the 'improvements' that were being made at the former arsenal, stating; 'the prisoners have been constantly employed for the benefit of the State.' Martin put in place a system of what he called 'humane but firm' discipline which relied on solitary confinement, bread and water or whipping for transgressors as well as 'chains, muskets, and bayonets [which] proved useful deterrents to escape attempts'.

Not everybody was as sanguine about the treatment of prisoners as the prison commandant.

As soon as July 1869, reports circulated concerning acts of cruelty committed against a white convict who had tried to escape (it is likely, in the South at that time, that nobody would have been as concerned about the prisoner if, like most of the inmates, he had been black).

The state governor, accompanied by the sheriff of local Gadsden County, visited the prison. He concluded that Martin was indeed a 'strict disciplinarian,' but that his sternness was tempered by his 'Irish heart.' A court of inquiry acquitted Martin of charges of cruelty to the prisoner in question, but the Irishman soon had reason to write to a newspaper in Jacksonville, setting out his defence of his methods and rejecting accusations of barbarity. Martin was also writing to friends, claiming that accusations of mismanagement and brutality were part of a campaign orchestrated by his political rivals to oust him from his job and install their own man.

However, there is clear evidence that Martin was already, barely a year into the job, feathering his own nest. He bought land near the prison and built a house in 1870, using prison labour. He began his own vineyard producing cheap wine, again using prison labour. There were already rumours flying that Martin and his men were making money, directly or indirectly, through the hard labour of prisoners and the state government acted, bringing in new laws which, amongst other measures, prohibited the 'employment of a Prisoner by any of the officers of the Prison for private or personal purposes.'

The politicians wanted to keep the Irishman on a tight leash, with semi-regular inspection visits and periodic attempts to limit his powers. They were not pioneering humanitarians; they were mostly concerned about the opportunities for corruption.

However, Martin was learning to play the political game. In 1872, while still warden, he was elected to the Florida House of Representatives for Gadsden County. He would go on to become the Speaker of the State legislature. In 1873, with a growing political base, Martin started to expand his farming enterprises and land holdings.

His main concern was the growing of grape vines to make a cheap wine called 'Scuppernong'. By the fall of 1874 he was producing two thousand gallons of wine per acre with a profit of thirty-five cents per gallon. His Hermitage vineyard could, conceivably, make him a small fortune, especially as his workforce were unpaid convicts, labouring from sun-up to sun-down.

Martin also had interests in logging and the production of turpentine, a dangerous and deeply-unpleasant job that took up large swathes of Florida's timber scrub. It was forced labour, in Florida's punishing climate, in hundreds of remote bush work-camps with little food, disease, no medical care, brutal conditions and whippings for any convict who dared break the rules. Once chained up in the system and working for gang bosses who had basically bought them as slaves and knew that they were plenty more where they came from, life-expectancy was not high.

Meanwhile, the Irishman was growing bolder, deliberately hiding the facts from his superiors or, in one case at least, ordering his guards to drive away, at bayonet point, a group of politicians who had come to inspect his prison.

However, Martin appears to have been a poor businessman and towards the end of his time at Chattahoochee, he wrote to one friend that if he failed to sell his property, he would be 'out on the world without a home or a dollar'. It is something of a mystery as to what Martin did with the money that he must have been able to skim off the convict-leasing system. With the post-war economy in Florida taking off, thanks to timber and turpentine production, road and railway building and other labour intensive activities, he would have been in a position to make a small fortune. The large timber, mining and railroad concerns leased hundreds of prisoners at a time. Fortunes were being made. But Malachi Martin was apparently not amongst those making them.

In 1877, after further investigations by the authorities which found that he had abused his position to put convicts to work on his own land, Martin lost his position as prison warder. The new, Democratic Party-led state government wanted this carpetbagger out and his public career began to wane as he failed to gain re-election to his seat in Gadsden County.

Martin continued to produce wine at his Hermitage vineyard, live on in his convict-built house at Mount Pleasant and work for the Republican Party. During the 1880 elections, he worked as an election inspector for his native county, a position that brought him into violent conflict with supporters of the Democratic Party.

In November and December 1880, Martin wrote a series of letters to the national Republican Party leader William Chandler, in which he complained of threats of violence against him by 'iniberated Democrats [sic]'.

He wrote:

'I have gone through a great deal of danger during political campaigns in Fla., but never in all my life have I been so near being assinated [sic] as on the night of the last election!'

'The Democrats say that if it was not for me they would have no difficulty in controlling the Niggers ... I am not particularly anxious to become a martyr or ... to make my wife a widow. Come what will I must leave here.'

At the time, many Southern Democrats would have regarded Martin, a Northerner, as an interfering blow-in and as representing everything they hated about the Yankees. He would have had many enemies, some of whom would be prepared to do him physical harm.

Martin practically begged for a Government job that would take him out of his perilous situation.

In another letter to a close friend around the same time, he bemoaned his position:

'I have been unable to sell my property and have rented all my farming lands to col'd men, except my home place and my vineyards. I am taking all the precautions I can, keep good dogs and a night watch man around my buildings. If they get me, there will be another funeral besides mine, unless they are quicker than I am.'

Those at the top of the Republican party must have felt some pity for the former war hero, he was appointed, in May 1881, to the job of state surveyor, although he continued with his vineyard business.

By this stage, Martin, who had remarried some years previously to a lady called Anna from Maine and had a daughter to go with his son from his first marriage, was in his early sixties, overweight and suffering from heart-disease. On 29 August 1884, aged sixty-two, Martin died at his home. At his own request, his body was shipped north to New York for burial in a Catholic graveyard on Long Island.

His family gradually sold off their lands and in 1912, his son Walter sold the last remaining tie to the Tallahassee area, the family home at Mount Pleasant. The former prison at Chattahoochee had been closed down shortly after Martin lost his job as warder and became the State 'insane asylum'.

The Convict Lease System, had, after his departure from the penal system, been refined, expanded and grown to the point where there were over thirty-five prison camps in Florida by 1899, containing thousands of men, women and even children. Towards the end of the nineteenth century, it became a massive revenue generator with thousands of convicts hired out to work in the fields, on the roads, on the railways and plantations.

Malachi Martin was just one part of the system. There is even evidence that he was concerned with the education and rehabilitation of convicts. But as a carpetbagger and man of his time, he profited (though never to the extent he could have) through the misery of others in a brutal regime that he was a significant part of. Other cleverer and more ruthless men, many of them sitting in private clubs and banking houses in New York, would make the millions that were to be had from the systematic and brutal exploitation of the poor, the ex-slaves, the unfortunates of Florida.

The last prison camps closed in Florida in 1924, but only after a series of scandals and gross miscarriages of justice.

Malachi Martin might have been as forgotten as the now derelict prison he ran at Chattahoochee if it wasn't for the book written by his former prison camp captain turned prison reform campaigner. That picture of him, as the archetypal, brutal prison warder, the father of the chain-gang, is the one that has endured.

BURKE AND HARE
THE RESURRECTION MEN

'Why, sir, bless your innocent eyebrows, that's where the mysterious
disappearance of a 'spectable tradesman took place four years ago.'
'You don't mean to say he was burked, Sam?' said Mr Pickwick,
looking hastily round.

The Pickwick Papers, Charles Dickens, 1837.

For generations of Scottish children, bad behaviour could raise the grotesque spectre of Burke and Hare, the wild Irish bogeymen who would come to strangle them in their sleep and sell their tiny corpses to be cut up on a cold, damp slab.

The arrest, in nineteenth-century Edinburgh, of the two Irish men and the gruesome revelations about their crimes provoked riots in the city, during which a mob burnt down the medical school that had been the final destination for their victims. And well into the twentieth century, long after their heinous crimes had passed into folk legend, children on the streets of Edinburgh would still sing a rhyme as they skipped rope:

Up the close and down the stair,
Back and forth with Burke and Hare,
Burke's the butcher, Hare's the thief,
Knox the boy who buys the beef.

Knox was a reference to the surgeon Professor Robert Knox, who asked no questions and paid good money for fresh corpses.

Burke and Hare were probably the most prolific Irish serial killers in history. They were also the most infamous. Their crimes were committed in an age when mass-market newspapers were just beginning to reach into every town and village and when, as now, nothing sold newsprint or excited the public interest so much as a grisly murder case.

The story of Burke and Hare would directly inspire tales from writers like Robert Louis Stevenson and Dylan Thomas and several movies, including one with the great horror stars Bela Lugosi and Boris Karloff. Charles Dickens references the Burke and Hare murders in *The Pickwick Papers* of 1837, using the grisly verb – 'to burke', meaning 'to smother' – that derived from the name and methods of William Burke.

The irony of Burke and his partner Hare becoming the most notorious 'Resurrection Men' – body snatchers who would disinter the recently deceased and sell their corpses to medical schools and surgeons for dissection – in history, was that the two Irishmen were never grave robbers in the accepted sense. They were simply too lazy and disorganised for the hard work of digging up corpses. William Burke and William Hare always found it easier to cut out the middle man and look after the dispatching of souls by themselves.

They accounted for at least sixteen and probably around thirty actual victims (due in part to the their targeting of transients who would not be missed, the true figure has never been established despite the posthumous discovery of fairly detailed accounts of bodies despatched and payments received by the brains of the operation, Burke).

The resurrection business was thriving in the early nineteenth century, fuelled by the march of science and the desire to learn more about the human body; in Britain and the United States, bodies were not made legally available for dissection, but medical schools needed a ready supply of cadavers for study and for teaching. Up until the 1760s, medical colleges in the UK were able to claim the bodies of recently-hanged criminals. But falling rates of execution and a growing public outrage about this 'unholy' practice (bad enough the sinner was hanged without their mortal remains ending up in jars to be gawked at by students), gradually closed off this supply. However, medical schools were flourishing and the laws of supply and demand meant an opening for those who were not too squeamish about handling the dead.

What arose was the ghoulish, illicit trade in fresh cadavers. Gangs of Resurrection Men would keep a close eye on the morgues and graveyards of the major cities; there was big money to be made, cadaver-hungry surgeons and medical colleges would pay up to ten pounds sterling for a fresh corpse in the 1820s in England, a huge sum for a night's work when the average labourer's pay was under twenty pounds a year.

Beggars, prostitutes, the very poor and those without family made for the easiest victims with many snatched right off the slab in the morgue for the cost of a few shillings or a naggin of whiskey to the right man. Such was the extent of the trade that the wealthy took extreme steps to protect their mortal remains. Many graves were sealed with heavy slabs of granite or marble to deter the Resurrectionists' picks and shovels. Others ringed their final resting places with high, spiked, wrought-iron rails or grates that can still be seen on and around some late-eighteenth and early-nineteenth century graves today. Glasnevin Cemetery on the north-side of Dublin city, for example, still retains its high walls and look-out towers, built to deter the body-snatchers. For decades, watchmen with bloodhounds would roam through the rows of tombstones and crosses at night, carrying torches and keeping guard to ensure that the recently entombed stayed that way.

For poorer families, the only protection against the body-snatchers was to stand guard over their loved-ones' graves for days, until their corpses were too ripe for harvesting.

Contemporary reports have gangs of Resurrection Men 'stalking the dead', following funeral processions, noting the place of burial and waiting for the family to drop their guard. A common trick was for the gangs to pay gravediggers to use ruses that would see the body placed in a shallow grave (one method was to use a false bottom in the coffin) for ease of removal. Some gangs would also employ tipsters to stalk the crowded lodging rooms, poor-houses and back alleys of crowded cities, keeping an eye out for those who were not long for this world. Once dead, their bodies would be snatched before family, friends or the authorities had the chance to claim them. And perhaps, once body snatchers started stalking the vulnerable and the seriously ill, it was only a matter of time before someone decided to give death a helping hand ...

The body-snatchers were operating in a legal limbo. A court in London in 1788, ruling on a charge of grave-robbing, had decided that as a body was not property, the theft of one could not be considered a crime. Strangely, the taking of the shroud or clothes covering a corpse was considered theft, so in many cases, horrified families turned up at the graves of recently deceased loved ones to find nothing but an open grave, a pried-off coffin lid and the box containing the vestments of the resurrected.

In some cases, the medical students took matters into their own hands and some colleges and schools earned a gruesome reputation for grave-robbing. In one incident in Aberdeenshire, Scotland in the early 1800s a medical student out grave-raiding was captured by cemetery watchmen and imprisoned in the watch-house. The student's friends did not desert him. They made off to the nearest public house and returned to ply the unsuspecting guard with a jug of whisky. As they drank and exchanged stories the imprisoned student burrowed his way through the roof of the house and escaped. The drunken guard spent the rest of the night guarding an empty room.

There were even reports in England of rival gangs of medical students coming to blows with pick-axes and crowbars in grave-yards in the early hours of the morning as they fought for possession of a freshly-buried corpse.

Such was the epidemic of grave-robbing from the 1770s to the 1830s that one British Prime Minister, Robert Peel, was moved to observe (in one of the more gratuitous puns in parliamentary history) that the theft of bodies had 'become a grave matter'. It would take decades of growing outrage, and the case of Burke and Hare, to finally push the authorities into combating the grisly trade of the Resurrection Men.

William Burke and William Hare would probably never have met were it not for the crippling poverty and great social upheavals seen in Ireland at the close of the eighteenth century.

Both men came from poor, rural backgrounds.

In one of his later confessions, William Burke gave a brief biography of himself to his interrogators, who noted: 'Burke is thirty-six years of age, was born in the parish of Orrey, County Tyrone (Ireland) in 1792; served seven years in the army, most of that time as an officer's servant in the Donegal Militia. He was married at Ballina, in the county of Mayo, when in the army, but left his wife and two children in Ireland. She would not come to Scotland with him. He has often wrote to her, but got no answer. He came to Scotland to work at the Union Canal, and wrought there while it lasted. He resided for about two years in Peebles, and worked as a labourer. He wrought as a weaver for eighteen months, and as a baker for five months. He learned to mend shoes, as a cobbler, with a man he lodged with in Leith.'

Burke had travelled to Scotland in around 1817, along with

thousands of other poor Irish labourers, who were drawn to the construction of the thirty-two mile long Union Canal.

They were known as 'navigators' (from which we get the term 'navvies'), rough, often desperate men who toiled from dawn to dusk, usually in brutal conditions, for a subsistence pay on the great construction projects of the era.

William Hare was born in 1792 (or possibly as late as 1804), with his birthplace variously given as Poyntzpass near Newry or Derry itself. Little is known of his life until he too moved to Scotland to work as a navvy on the Union Canal. He was said by one newspaper report of the time to be known since his youth as 'always remarkable for being of a ferocious and malignant disposition'. Hare was said to have fled Ireland after flogging one of his employer's horses to death.

After his time on the Union, which links Edinburgh to Falkirk and the Forth and Clyde Canal, he moved to the city of Edinburgh where he met and befriended a man called Logue, the owner of a boarding house in the poor West Port area of the city.

When Logue died in 1826, Hare married his widow, Margaret, and ran the boarding house with her while also occasionally working as a navvy.

Unlike his more educated partner in crime, Hare left no real record of himself and we have to depend on the account of a man who met him, after he was charged with his crimes, given to *Blackwood's Magazine* of Edinburgh in 1829.

The witness writes of Hare being 'the most brutal man ever

subjected to my sight, and at first look seemingly an idiot. [His face] when he laughed – which he did often – collapsed into a hollow, shooting up ghastlily from chin to cheek bone – all steeped in a sullenness and squalor ... native to the almost deformed face of the leering miscreant ... so utterly loathsome was the whole look of the reptile.'

The account may be a little biased. By the time it was given, Hare was one half of the most notorious duo of killers and body-snatchers of the era. There were mobs baying for their blood in the streets of Edinburgh.

However, it was only by a quirk of fate that the two Irishmen had met and fallen into the business of killing. Both heavy drinkers and gamblers, they were motivated by the need for easy money, a total lack of moral scruples and a ready supply of victims. While William Burke was lodging at the village of Maddiston, near Falkirk, on the Union Canal, he met with a native Scots woman called Helen McDougal, who had separated from her husband and was then living with a man with whom she had two children. Helen must have seen something in the navvy from Donegal. Shortly after they met, she left her partner and their children and travelled with Burke to several small towns before they ended up in Edinburgh. It was a very hard life, with the couple scraping by on casual work on farms, in bakeries, selling old clothes and mending shoes wherever they could.

It was in Edinburgh, living in rooms in the West Port district, that Burke and McDougal met with Margaret Logue, now living as Margaret Hare, wife of William. Soon after, Burke and McDougal became paying lodgers of the Hares at Tanner's Close in West Port, a crowded district of poor people living in filthy lanes and ramshackle tenements and flophouses. The two couples were never described as friends. Witnesses later told of how they would regularly have blazing rows that often spilled into the crowded streets of West Port. But they did share a fondness for whiskey and for high living on easy money.

On 27 November 1827, a cold Edinburgh night, Burke and Hare hit upon the scheme that would link their names together forever.

An elderly lodger of Hare's known as Old Donald had died, owing him £4 in rent. Hare felt cheated out of his money and discussed the matter with Burke. Both men had heard rumours that certain medical men of the city were prepared to pay good money for fresh corpses and they decided on a way that Old Donald could pay back his debt. On the day of the funeral, the two men removed Old Donald's corpse from his coffin, filling it with old bits of wood so as to ensure it still had a bit of weight.

Through criminal contacts, they knew of a Professor Robert Knox at Surgeon's Square who was always on the lookout for fresh cadavers. They took the body to Knox and were paid £7 and ten shillings for it. For the two Irishmen, it must have seemed the easiest of easy money. Knox, for his part, told them that he was always in the market for a good corpse, if one should come their way again. The two couples celebrated their windfall in high style, toasting Old Donald and his honourable – if late – payment of debts. But the money did not last long and as the courts later heard from Burke himself, it was the hunger for more easy money that 'made them try the murdering for subjects'.

From January through October 1828, Burke and Hare, with the certain collusion of their two women, killed at least three men, twelve women and one child.

Their first victim was another lodger, Joseph Miller, who took ill in December of 1827. Burke and Hare waited for the Grim Reaper to do his job, but when death proved to be tardy and Miller showed signs of making a full recovery, the two men took matters into their own hands. They hit upon their proven method for dispatching victims. They would usually ply the unsuspecting target with drink and hospitality. Then, one man, usually Hare, would pinion the victim, often by sitting on his or her chest, while the other would clamp his hands over the mouth and nose. It would become known as 'burking'. They reckoned this form of strangulation would not leave any incriminating marks or wounds on the bodies and they could claim that the person had simply died in their sleep. The method also had the happy affect of preserving relatively fresh and intact bodies for the medical students. Their first murder victim, Miller, went off to the anatomist, Knox, and the easy money made convinced the Irish duo that they had hit on the perfect crime.

In an age when death really did stalk the poor at every turn, they could count on a sudden spike in the mortality rate in Tanner's Close going unnoticed. At first, Burke and Hare did make some efforts to cover their tracks, picking on victims who were not particularly well-known in the locality and were unlikely to have many friends and family who might ask awkward questions, but their greed and laziness soon got the better of them and they became sloppy.

The court that eventually tried them heard evidence from witnesses that they had even considered killing their own women, Helen and Margaret, if they ever ran short of money.

As Burke and Hare set off on their killing spree, there was always a willing customer in the shape of Professor Robert Knox, a keen scientist and anatomist although, as it turned out later, he was largely a self-taught 'surgeon'. Knox would later claim complete ignorance of the murders, but he surely must have wondered about the two Irishmen who appeared to have an unending stream of fresh corpses for him. Even to a myopic man of science, many aspects of the trade must have struck him as odd: some of the bodies had been hastily stuffed into a bag, box or even an old tea-chest for delivery. None showed signs of having been in the ground, one or two were even still warm (according to medical students who were later called to give evidence). None of this seemed to bother Knox. And if he ever had concerns about the two men he later called 'Celtic thugs', he appears to have kept them to himself.

This reluctance to ask questions may have been connected to the profits that Knox himself was making through the high fees paid by gentlemen medical students who were anxious to have a cut off a fresh corpse themselves. The good doctor once declared; 'I would rather be the discoverer of one fact in science than have a fortune bestowed upon me.' He was fortunate to have, through the murderous activities of Burke and Hare, the chance to have both the science and the shillings.

In February of 1827, Burke and Hare despatched a local woman called Abigail Simpson and a man known only in the subsequent court records as an 'English Peddler'.

Their crimes followed an established, if haphazard, pattern. They would stalk and 'burke' their victim, deliver the body to Knox and then drink and laze about the lodging house for days until the money began to run out. When it did, they started looking around for a warm body.

Few questions were asked. They could depend on Knox to keep quiet, even if he must have been deeply suspicious, and they almost always targeted the old or the vulnerable, marginal, street people who nobody would care enough about to wonder about their disappearance.

They might have continued in their trade for years if it wasn't for two murders in particular that almost invited detection. One was of a local, disabled boy, a harmless, much-loved street entertainer known as 'Daft Jamie' (his real name was James Wilson, a mentally-retarded seventeen-year-old).

Hare came across Jamie as he was out on the streets of Edinburgh on a cold October night in 1828. The young man was lost and looking for his mother. The Irishman told him that he knew where his mother was and to follow him to her.

Daft Jamie was brought to the lodging house and offered whiskey by Burke and his woman. When he refused more than a small drop, he was offered a warm bed for the night until they brought his mother to him.

Jamie was soon asleep and Burke moved in to smother him in the usual fashion. However, the boy woke up and tried to fight to save his life. Burke screamed to Hare for help and the two men eventually managed to smother the life out of the harmless young man.

They had another body, sold for a healthy £15 because of an interesting deformity to one of the feet, but they had made a serious mistake. The disappearance of Daft Jamie, a constant fixture on the streets of West Port, would not go unnoticed.

Neither would the earlier disappearance of a young, very pretty 'street-girl' known as Mary Paterson, characterised at the time as a teenage prostitute with many friends and admirers.

On 9 April 1828, Mary Paterson was lured to a house rented by William Burke's brother in Gibb's Close in the Canongate, with her friend Janet Brown.

The trial of Burke later heard that Mary passed out with drink, but Janet, sensing that something was not quite right, excused herself, saying she would return later for her friend. On her return, Janet was told that Mary and Burke had gone out but she insisted on waiting. Meanwhile, she had confided her concerns to her landlady, Mrs Lawrie, who became worried and sent a servant to tell Janet to leave immediately.

The body of Mary Paterson had actually been in the house all of the time, bundled into a back room and covered up with straw. Her friend Janet, by asking questions, had almost met a similar fate.

Mary's corpse was soon on its way to Knox's anatomy school in Surgeon's Square; the professor was particularly delighted with his new acquisition and preserved the body of the beautiful young teenager in a barrel of whiskey for three months before he could finally bring himself to dissect it. The whiskey was said by some to have ended up in a local public house. The good doctor even brought in a number of local artists to sketch and capture the beauty of his young specimen.

When the story of Mary Paterson's grisly end was finally made public, the teenage girl achieved a sort of macabre celebrity that was by turns sentimental, cautionary and titillating. The Scottish writer and artist Charles Kirkpatrick Sharpe caught the public mood, saying of Mary Paterson, 'She was a person of disorderly life, and is said to have been well known to Burke before he murdered her … She was cut short in her sinful career, and hurried (O, dreadful thought – how much unprepared!) before the judgement-seat of her offended Maker.'

Mary Paterson and her 'sinful career' may have made a good morality tale for the times, but recent research into the Burke and Hare murders has uncovered intriguing evidence that as well as being murdered, Mary saw her reputation unjustly blackened. It is a story that might resonate with our own times.

It seems that Mary Paterson, the beautiful teenage 'street-girl' and victim of Burke and Hare may not have been a prostitute at all, as some of her outraged friends protested at the time of her death. The historian and writer Lisa Rosner has found evidence in the Edinburgh archives that Paterson was not a professional prostitute, but rather a resident of a Magdalene Asylum, a home for 'fallen' young girls of the type that was still operating in Ireland up to the 1960s. It is possible that Paterson met Burke shortly after being released from the strict confines of the Magdalene Asylum, a place of hard work and Bible study. These new facts paint a very different picture of the most famous victim of the infamous Burke and Hare.

Burke and Hare considered women easier 'marks' than men who might try to fight their way out of their clutches. Another victim, Ann McDougal, was a relative of Burke's woman, Helen, who had again been lured in with promises of a warm bed and a dram of whiskey. And while Burke had no qualms about killing her, he did ask that Hare do the deed. The woman was, after all, family.

Mary Halden, a prostitute, was lured to Hare's boarding house. When her young teenage daughter, Peggy, called looking for her, she was taken aside by Hare. Mother and daughter ended up dead and delivered to Professor Knox where they fetched ten pounds each.

Mary and Peggy were well known in the area and gossip soon

started running through the streets of West Port. Blow-ins and transients might just simply disappear. But what had happened to the mother and daughter who were seen every day on the streets around their home?

Burke and Hare could have lain low, but they became, in fact, even more careless and decided that their next victim would be James Wilson, the young man with a deformed foot who made his living as a children's entertainer. When Daft Jamie's body was delivered up to Knox and laid on the dissecting table, several of his startled young students immediately recognised him by his distinctive, deformed foot. Knox blustered that they must be mistaken – but he began his lecture by dissecting the corpse's face.

On Halloween night 1828 Mary Docherty, the sixteenth and final victim, was killed after Burke and his partner, Helen, had convinced her to stay with them at their lodgings. The couple had persuaded the elderly Irish woman that they were relatives who only wanted to offer her a roof over her head.

It was around this time that Burke and his common-law wife fell out with the Hares over their suspicions that they were selling bodies to Knox behind their backs and left the lodging house. Another couple, James and Ann Gray, had been staying next to their rooms and became suspicious when the elderly Irish woman suddenly disappeared.

The Grays were told that Mary had been asked to leave because she had become 'overly friendly' with Burke. But the grim truth was that she was still in the house, dead and thrust under the bed in the spare room with a covering of straw. The Grays became suspicious when they were sternly warned not go to into the room. They discovered the body and immediately confronted Helen who panicked and offered them ten pounds to keep quiet. The Grays went off to report the body to the police. By the time the constables arrived, the body had already been spirited away to Surgeon's Square. It was later found there and identified by James Gray.

Burke and Hare and their two women were all arrested and questioned separately. The men immediately began blaming each other while the women, in turn, blamed the men and claimed to have no knowledge of the crimes.

A month of questioning brought the police no closer to getting to the bottom of what had happened. And there was an obvious problem with the physical evidence. Seldom has the legal term *Habeas Corpus* (or 'produce the body') carried so much irony in a courtroom.

Finally, the exasperated Lord Advocate, Sir William Rae, offered Hare immunity to turn King's Evidence and testify against Burke and Helen. Hare immediately agreed to do so, knowing that he would escape the noose while his former friend and partner would surely hang.

The short trial at the High Court of Justiciary began on Christmas Eve 1828 and on Christmas Day, Burke and Helen were charged with the murder of Mary Docherty.

Burke alone was also charged with the murder of Mary Paterson and James Wilson and sentenced to death by hanging. Helen's part in the crimes was 'not proven' and she was freed.

On 28 January 1829 over twenty-five thousand people attended and cheered the hanging of William Burke in the Lawnmarket in Edinburgh. Many had already been part of a mob that had attacked and burned the medical school where the killers had taken the victims.

In a final irony for Burke, his body ended up being dissected in anatomy lectures. Some of the students removed pieces of his skin and used it to bind a small handbook. Today, that book is kept in a collection of medical oddities housed at the Surgeons' Hall Museum in Edinburgh. The cover, made from Burke's tightly-stretched skin, bears the words 'EXECUTED 28 JAN 1829' and 'BURKE'S SKIN POCKET BOOK' in faded gilt lettering. Nearby, visitors can also see Burke's skeleton with his death mask, and the life mask of Hare. Before he was cut up on the slab, Burke's body was put on public exhibition and thousands of people streamed passed. One observer put the flow at sixty persons per minute.

There was much public anger that William Hare had been let off. But despite further efforts to prosecute him, including a civil case brought by the mother of James Wilson, he was released in February 1829 and escaped to England via the postal coach.

Hare is said to have been later recognised in England and flung into a pit of quick-lime, which left him blind. A report in the *Newry Telegraph* of March 1829 also claimed he had been attacked by a mob of people there after trying to return home. Hare faded from public notoriety and is said to have died a blind beggar in London, some years later.

The two women in their lives, Helen and Margaret, found it impossible to stay in Scotland, being mobbed everywhere they went. It is rumoured that Helen escaped to Australia, where she died in 1868. Margaret is said to have fled to Ireland after nearly being lynched by a mob in Glasgow.

Professor Knox, who asked no questions, also found it impossible to stay in Edinburgh and relocated to London, where he worked in a cancer hospital until the end of his days. He was acquitted for his part in the murders. Knox did try to cash in on his notoriety, setting himself up as an expert lecturer on the criminal mind. He based his lectures (and a number of books he published) on the tendency of some races, most notably the 'Celtic thug' to commit dastardly crimes that could fool even the most high-minded and superior Saxons.

However, any hopes that he had of a successful career as a celebrity scientist came to naught.

The Burke and Hare case did lead directly to a change in the law. The Warburton Anatomy Act was introduced shortly after their trial. It properly criminalised grave-robbing and regularised the supply of corpses to medical schools (they would mostly be the unclaimed remains of the poor and the destitute, often from workhouses or hospitals).

The era of the grave-snatchers was over. It was buried with

Burke and Hare.

★ ★ ★

In 1829 a notebook was discovered in a tin box buried under a flagstone near Burke's house. It seems that William Burke kept a written record and account of the murders and the money he made. It states:

Left the Donnegal militia and came to Edinburgh, December 1818, to follow the shoemaker trade.

1 Sept 1826 – Went to lodge with Hare, Tanner's Close, and assisted with the cuddy.

Christmas 1827 – Sold the body of Donald the pensioner, in Surgeon Square, for £ 7,10.

Paid William Hare, Tanner's Close, £ 4,5.

For myself, £ 3,5.

April 2 – Sold the woman from Gilmerton for £ 9.

Paid William Hare foresaid, £ 4.

Paid a porter 5.

Drank 3. 3d. a box is.

For myself £ 4, 10s.

May 7 – Sold the old woman, who came to lodge in Tanner's Close, and the child, for £ 12.

Paid for drink, porterage, &c. 7s. Paid William Hare £ 5.

For myself £ 6, 13.

July 1 – Sold the Englishman for £ 10. Kept the whole money, for

Hare's conduct to me.

22 – Sold the woman Haldane for £ 6. Paid Hare, being due him £ 5.

Paid Donald the porter, being jealous of him £ 1.

Aug 2 – Sold the old woman, and her grand daughter for £ 11. Paid Hare £ 5.

Paid the grocer for a herring barrel 1s. 6d, whisky and Donald 7, 6J.

For myself £ 5, 15, 61.

Oct 5 – Sold the girl Paterson for £ 10, which was all paid to Hare, he being hard up.

31 – Sold James Wilson, or Daft Jamie for £ 15.

★ ★ ★

A Note on the origins of Hare from the *Newry Telegraph*, 31 March 1829

Hare the Murderer

On Friday evening last Hare the murderer called in a public house in Scarva accompanied by his wife and child and having ordered a naggin of whiskey he began to enquire for the welfare of every member of the family of the house, with well affected solicitude. However, as Hare is a native of this neighbourhood, he was very soon recognised and ordered to leave the place immediately, with which he complied after attempting to palliate his horrid crimes by describing them as having been the effects of intoxication. He took the road towards Loughbrickland followed by a number of boys yelling and threatening in such a manner as obliged him to take through the fields with such speed that he soon disappeared whilst his unfortunate wife remained on the road imploring forgiveness and denying, in the most solemn manner, any participation in the crimes of her wretched husband. They now reside at the house of an uncle of Hare's near Loughbrickland. Hare was born and bred about one half mile distant from Scarva in the opposite county of Armagh and shortly before his departure from this country he lived in the service of Mr Hall, the keeper of the eleventh lock near Poyntzpass. He was chiefly engaged in driving the horses which his master employed in hauling lighters on the Newry Canal. He was always remarkable for being of a ferocious and malignant disposition, an instance of which he gave in the killing of one of his Master's horses, which obliged him to fly to Scotland where he perpetrated those unparalleled crimes that must always secure him a conspicuous page in the annals of murder. [Correspondence of *The Northern Whig*]

VINCENT 'MAD DOG' COLL
ORIGINAL GAEILGEOIR GANGSTER. MOB HITMAN AND CHILD-KILLER

Vincent Coll was, in some ways, a man born out of his time. In the seventeenth and eighteenth century, young Irishmen who displayed a talent for killing, plunder and betrayal were as likely to be celebrated in ballads and rewarded by kings as hung from the nearest gallows. In his brief but blazing career as a killer, bootlegger, kidnapper, shake-down artist, hijacker and hit-man-for-hire, the young man labelled 'Mad Dog' and 'Child Killer' by a mayor of New York, more than earned his place amongst the most notorious Irishmen in history.

Coll, who was born in Donegal in 1908, was a killer that even the Mafia feared. He might not have been much of a student of the past, but if the young Vincent had paid attention to the Irish priests in the Catholic Reform Schools of New York, or heard on the streets of the Bronx about the history of Irish gangs of the Five Points, Hell's Kitchen and beyond, he might have seen himself as the last expression of a long and bloody tradition. The Irish were the original gangsters of New York. Before the villages of Southern Italy and the Tsarist ghettoes began to pour forth their tired, poor and huddled masses, Irish immigrants in New York ran much of the criminal enterprise of the early-to-mid-nineteenth century in

America's most populous city. The exotically named Irish gangs of New York included the Whyos, the Dead Rabbits (who marched through the notorious Five Points carrying pikes adorned with skewered rabbits), the Shirt Tails, Gorillas, Plug Uglies, The Parlour Mob and the Kerrytonians. In districts like the notorious Hell's Kitchen, huddled around the Hudson River Docks on the West Side of Manhattan, the Irish (together with gangs that grew out of German immigrant communities) represented a constant threat to civil order in the city.

In the infamous Draft Riots of July 1863, Irish mobs rampaged through Manhattan in what started out as a protest against the draft imposed on behalf of the Union Army, then fighting the South in the Civil War. By the time some sort of order had been imposed after three days of mayhem, upwards of two thousand people had been killed and eight thousand wounded. It had degenerated into a racial pogrom with mobs attacking African-American men, women and children in the streets. One Irish mob burnt down an orphanage for black children on Fifth Avenue and Forty-Second Street, (fortunately, the 233 children inside had a miraculous escape). The Army was forced to use artillery and fixed bayonets to clear the streets.

The New York Orange Riots of 1870 and 1871 were a purely Irish affair, nationalist Catholics against Irish Protestant Orangemen who had tried to march up Eighth Avenue in New York to mark the anniversary of the Battle of the Boyne. In 1870, the parade descended into violence that left eight dead. As a result, the New York City authorities moved to ban the 1871 parade, but were accused by a coalition of powerful interest groups, including Wall Street businessmen, the Protestant Church and a number of newspaper barons, of giving in to the growing power of the radical Irish Catholics. There were claims that the Papist Irish, together with their priests and bishops, were planning to emulate the radical Paris Commune takeover of the French capital, which had been put down just two months before. The parade went ahead in July 1871; pitched battles between Catholics and Protestants, city police, the National Guard and State Militia (including cavalry units) raged up and down Eighth and Fifth Avenues and at least fifty people were killed. When the fighting was over, there were huge funeral processions through the Irish Catholic stronghold of Brooklyn, where the Governor was burned in effigy and sympathetic newspapers carried inflammatory headlines about the 'The Slaughter on Eighth Avenue'.

The riots meant the end for the Irish Protestant William Magear Tweed, the infamous 'Boss Tweed' of Tammany Hall, the Democratic Party political machine which effectively controlled the city and the State. Tammany Hall, also known as the Society of St Tammany, was the New York political organisation behind the Democratic Party in the City and State, with its headquarters in the original Tammany Hall on East 14th Street in Manhattan from 1830. It had started out as a political society for 'native' Americans, but with the arrival of the Irish, who quickly seized control, it became strongly identified with the control and exercise of political power, patronage and graft on behalf of the Democratic party and the proud Sons of Erin in New York. It also became a byword for political corruption.

Tweed had been allowed to control the reins of power by the leading citizens of the city because of his supposed ability to maintain stability. As one leading protestant minister pointed out immediately after the Orange Riots, Tweed had 'failed to keep the Irish in line'.

Of course, not all the Irish needed 'keeping in line'. They had been arriving in their hundreds of thousands, even before the Famine. And like many immigrant groups, they gradually became part of their adopted city and began to organise politically, securing power and influence in city and state politics, in the police and fire departments and other areas of the New York power structure. However, at the same time, the criminal gangs who controlled gambling, prostitution, the protection-rackets and other enterprises, would continue to grow with the Big Apple.

The Irish gangs were in many ways a response to the social and economic obstacles facing them on arrival in New York, where they found themselves right at the bottom of the food chain when it came to jobs and political influence (if we don't include the African-American slaves of the era before the Civil War). Before the War Between the States and the rapid expansion to the West, the Irish were compelled to gang up together to get their own slice of the crowded Big Apple. And if the 'nativist' political structure wouldn't give them an even break, they would take one for themselves. But by the time Vincent Coll arrived in New York, just one year old and with a large family who hoped to escape the grinding poverty of the Irish-speaking district of Gweedore in north Donegal, his countrymen were beginning to move off the bottom rung; the Irish in the city were changing, gaining respectability, leaving the crowded tenements and finding space in the new sub-urbs growing up around the city as the early 1900s brought fresh waves of immigrants, from Italy, Eastern and Central Europe and Tsarist Russia and Poland to the city. Coll and his family would never get the chance to join this move towards new horizons. The youngster would become associated with one of the remnants of the earlier days of New York when he ended up running with a venerable Irish street gang called the Gophers. With the Irish now associated with business, local government, the NYPD and the Fire Department and moving towards respectability, Vincent would make his name amongst the next generation of criminals, the Jewish and Italian gangsters who made prohibition-era New York rattle to the sound of the Tommy gun.

The Jews and Italians would have had to carve out their own territory in New York. And just as the Irish had done before them, most worked hard, organised their communities, gave their chil-dren whatever education they could afford and sought out the American Dream. Some choose a quicker route to prosperity. And the nexus point for Jewish, Italian and Irish criminals were gangs like Murder, Incorporated, the name given by the press to what criminal figures also called The Brownsville Boys or The Com-bination, a loose affiliation of Irish, Jewish and Italian hitmen-for-hire. In the popular narrative of the Gangster era, the Irish provided the muscle while the Italians and Jews ran the show. But in reality, the times offered equal opportunities for men of all ethnic backgrounds to find a niche based on their particular skill-sets. Some gangsters with Irish backgrounds, like Owney Madden, boss of Hell's Kitchen, would rise to the top and even achieve a certain sort of glamour (Madden ran the famous Cotton Club in New York). Some Jewish crime figures, like Mendy Weiss, were out-and-out killers. And some, such as Benjamin 'Bugsy' Siegel, would combine killing with upper-management responsibilities.

New York in the Prohibition era was a hot-house for criminal activity. The Federal Government was trying to enforce a deeply-unpopular, virtually-unworkable law banning the sale of alcohol.

Most state and local politicians, police chiefs, business leaders and opinion makers believed the Volstead Act to be, at best, an unenforceable law that simply pushed regular citizens into the arms of criminals. For the nascent criminal networks of the US, prohibition was sent from heaven to make them incredibly rich and powerful, putting them at the centre of a web of crime and influence involving ordinary citizens, corrupt politicians, police-men and lawyers.

Vincent Coll, with his personality and skills, was in the right place at the right time.

He had been born Uinseann Ó Colla on 20 July 1908 above a pub in Gweedore, north Donegal (the pub, Tígh Hiúdaí Beag, would be the future home of the family that gave us the famous Irish music groups Clannad and Altan). Long after his death, Uinseann, the infamous local boy gone bad across the sea, would be known to the people of that part of Donegal as '*An Madra Mire*', Irish for 'The Mad Dog'.

When Vincent was not quite a year old his father, Toaly Coll, decided to move the family, his wife and seven children, to New York in search of a better life. That better life never happened for the Colls. After settling in the Bronx in 1909, they remained trapped in dire poverty. Five of Vincent's six siblings died before he was twelve. His mother died of TB in 1916, worn out after years of trying to provide for her children. Vincent's father, Toaly, had simply run off years before and was never heard from again.

Needless to say, in such an unforgiving world, Vincent was fighting for his life almost from the moment he could walk the streets of the Bronx. He grew up quickly and he grew up mean. After his mother's death, his surviving sister did try to raise him in a cold-water flat on 11th Avenue, but she died when Vincent was eleven, leaving Vincent and his older brother Peter as the only survivors of the seven siblings. Vincent was then taken in by an elderly Irish woman, a neighbour, who treated him like her son.

Run-ins with the law were almost inevitable. Vincent soon developed a reputation for being a wild child of the streets and began the first of several stints in Catholic Reform School before he reached his teens. He was facing a murder charge by nineteen, but that was 'fixed' by the crime boss he then worked for. The ability to make problems with the law go away with dirty money was a lesson that Vincent learned early in his career.

Before prohibition, the Irish gangs dominated the Bronx and Manhattan, but during the prohibition era the mobs were increasingly Italian and Jewish and controlled by the likes of Dutch Schultz, the 'Bootlegger King of the Bronx' (real name Arthur Flegenheimer), Charlie 'Lucky' Luciano, Bugsy Siegel and Louis Lepke. Schultz was the son of a bar-keeper who built up an empire of speakeasies, clandestine alcohol-stills and breweries during the early years of prohibition. In a tough business, with rival gangs constantly trying to carve out their own territory, Schultz needed ruthless, violent young men with a talent for intimidation and killing. Vincent Coll had all of that in spades and started out as an enforcer for Schultz, when he was still in his mid-teens.

By now Vincent and his older brother, Peter, were beginning to make names for themselves in the Bronx. Vincent was the good-looking one, fresh-faced (some newspaper reports would later call him 'baby-faced' or endow him with 'matinee-idol' looks), with blond, curly hair, a fondness for sharp suits and an enigmatic, menacing air. He spent small fortunes on his clothes, which were stashed with various girlfriends across Manhattan and the Bronx. He favoured tailored suits, silk shirts, double-breasted Chesterfield overcoats and his signature hat, a pearl-grey fedora, always worn at a rakish angle. It was often said of Vincent that he had an ability to appear or disappear at will. He was a womaniser who always had a girl with a quiet apartment somewhere if he needed to lie low. Coll could be charming or taciturn as the situation demanded and was said to have a magnetic effect on women.

Right from the start of his career as a gangster, Coll displayed a maverick, independent streak that would enrage the powerful bosses he was supposed to be working for. Coll was never the classic 'soldier'. If anything, he was a gun for hire who always had his own angles to work. His real pleasure was kidnapping. And as you would expect from a gangster already known to his associates as 'The Mad Mick', he loved a challenge. Coll would kidnap wealthy citizens if the chance arose, but he took an almost perverse pleasure in the insanely risky business of kidnapping fellow gangsters and racketeers.

Two cases illustrate Coll's love of a challenge. The first concerned Owney 'The Killer' Madden: long after his death, NYC Police files revealed that Coll had been paid $35,000 for the safe return of Madden's business associate George 'Big Frenchy' DeMange in the summer of 1931. The money was paid over, but Madden may not have been pleased to see the Irishman then spending some of his money in his own nightclub, The Cotton Club, or parading down Broadway with chorus girls on his arm.

In a second case, Coll demanded another $45,000 to give up George Immerman, brother of Connie Immerman, the famous Harlem night club impresario and racketeer. The Donegal-born gangster must have known that there were easier ways to make a buck than targeting the most dangerous men in New York, along with their families and associates, but right from the start of his career, Vincent had shown zero respect for power or the established pecking order.

As rum-runners working for Dutch Schultz in the mid-twenties, the young Coll brothers were on $150 dollars a week. It was big money for ghetto kids, but Vincent saw their jobs as mere stepping stones. While working for The Dutchman, Vincent set about learning the bootlegging trade and tried to talk some of his fellow bootleggers and enforcers into splitting with Schultz and going into business for themselves (with Vincent in charge, naturally). As part of his scheme, Coll reached out to a Schultz soldier called Vincent Barelli, arranging a meet through his girlfriend, a girl called Mary Smith, who was the sister of a young man called Carmine Smith, a school-friend of the Colls in the Bronx. The meet did not go well. Barelli refused to betray Dutch Schultz so Vincent shot him dead. As Mary Smith was a witness, she got a bullet to the head as well. Vincent then decided it was time to make his move on his boss. In the spring of 1931, he told Schultz, one of the most powerful crime lords in New York, that he wanted a percentage of the business. Schultz refused.

'I don't take in nobody as partners with me,' he was said to have told the young Irishman. 'You're an ambitious punk, but you take a salary or nothing. Take it or leave it.'

'Okay', said Coll, with his familiar toothy grin, 'I'm leaving it.'

The result was all-out war. Two Irish brothers, Vincent and Peter, against the King of the Bronx and his army. The Colls went on the rampage, hijacking Schultz's delivery trucks, shooting his associates and burning out his speakeasies. Schultz could never lay a finger on Vincent; he was just too cunning and too good at hiding himself in the urban jungle. His brother Peter, on the other hand, could be got to. On 30 May 1931, Schultz's men cornered twenty-four-year-old Peter on a street corner in Harlem and he was killed in a hail of bullets.

Vincent Coll, the Mad Mick, went into a rage of grief and vengeance. Over the next three weeks, he gunned down four of Schultz's men. In all, around twenty men were killed in the blood-letting; the exact figure is hard to pin down as New York was also in the midst of the vicious Castellammarese War at the same time. It was mayhem on the streets of Manhattan and the police often had difficulty in deciding which corpse belonged to which war.

Coll was seriously out-gunned and tried to even the odds by paying top dollar to freelance hitmen to take out his targets. He raised the money by kidnapping and by trying to muscle in on other rackets, including those run by Jack 'Legs' Diamond (an Irishman who started out as Jack Nolan) and Owney 'The Killer' Madden. The Irishman was effectively running a protection racket on the racketeers. Even amongst the criminal underworld of New York, Coll was now an outlaw. To be even suspected of running with Coll could bring a death sentence. Dutch Schultz was deter-mined to kill his former employee. In the summer of 1931 he took the highly unusual step of walking into a police station in the Bronx and loudly declaring, 'I'll give a house in Westchester to any cop who can kill the Mick'.

On 28 July 1931, Vincent Coll was at the centre of a terrible incident that would see him labelled a 'child-killer' and shock even the war-weary citizens of New York. Coll had tracked down a

Schultz associate called Joey Rao and several of his men and went after them on a street in Spanish Harlem as they stood outside a social club tied to Dutch Schultz. Coll opened fire with his Tommy-gun while an associate opened up with a pump-action shotgun, but the spray of bullets missed their intended target and instead hit a group of children who were playing in the street. Five children were hit in the crossfire and one, five-year-old Michael Vengalli, died of terrible gunshot wounds to the stomach.

New York City Mayor Jimmy Walker dubbed Coll a 'Mad Dog' and a 'child-killer' and directed the police to treat him as Public Enemy Number One. Even Vincent Coll realised that he had gone too far. With the police and half the underworld of New York now closing in on him, he hit on a bold strategy. He kidnapped yet another one of Owney Madden's henchmen and collected a $30,000 ransom. Vincent needed the money to finance his plan and he needed to move fast as there was now a reputed $50,000 bounty on his head. The Irishman had managed to unite the biggest crime figures in New York – Dutch Schultz, Lucky Luciano, Legs Diamond, Owney Madden and Meyer Lansky – in their determination to rub out the Mad Dog. The Mafia, too, had decided that Coll was out of control and making too many waves. Gunning down gangland rivals in the street was one thing. But the violent death of children created the kind of heat that was seriously bad for business.

As the net closed in, Coll broke cover and effectively handed himself over to the police: the *New York Times* of 5 October 1931 reported the seizure of Coll and his gang at a house in upstate New York as a triumph for fearless detectives, but crime-historians believe that it was Coll himself who was ultimately behind the tip-off that led thirty policemen to his rented hide-out. Coll had grown a moustache and dyed his hair to disguise himself. But the photographs taken shortly after the arrest show him in his trade-mark pearl-grey fedora. The photos taken at the Bathgate Police station in the Bronx, where Coll was taken to be charged with the murder of five-year-old Michael Vengalli, show a relaxed and well-dressed Coll smiling for the cameras, next to his more dishevelled-looking, but still grinning, associate Frank Giordani.

The Mad Dog could afford to look relaxed even as the entire city bayed for his blood. He had a plan. Coll declared his inno-cence and used his ransom loot to hire the greatest defence lawyer of the age, Sam Leibowitz, to defend him in court.

Coll and his associates were paraded in front of a large crowd of newsmen, gawkers and over two hundred policemen, including New York City Police Commissioner Edward P. Mulrooney and Chief Inspector John J. Sullivan, when they were formally charged in the gymnasium at Police Headquarters in the early hours of 5 October.

Vincent wore a pearl grey suit, blue shirt, dark tie and Chesterfield overcoat with a blue handkerchief poking out of the breast pocket. He confirmed his identity and gave his profession as 'unemployed brick-layer'.

The *New York Times* noted the 'swagger of the young thug' and reported how he answered all questions related to the murder charges with, 'I will answer that when I see my counsel'. The charges were put to them by Chief Inspector John J. Sullivan, the archetypal New York Irish cop, finally face to face with the most notorious Irish gangster of the era. Inspector Sullivan addressed the prisoners and the crowd, all lit up in the glare of harsh floodlights, through a booming public address system.

'Coll, there, is a big gangster,' said Sullivan in what the *New York Times* reported was 'a voice with increasing contempt'.

'He's a brave fellow, he let a girl claim ownership of the gun found in his room. When I asked him where he got the gun and whose was it, he put it on her. That's the type of brave young fellow he is.'

'There's no doubt about it you're going away, Coll,' said Inspector Sullivan, turning directly to his fellow Irishman.

'You're responsible for killing that child. You're about as low and despicable as we ever get here.

'See!' [said Sullivan, now addressing the crowd] 'He's changed the colour of his hair and plucked his eyebrows and raised a moustache! Oh, you boys will go all right. Get out of here!'

The trial of Coll and his associates opened on 16 December 1931 in New York. It should have been a foregone conclusion, but Leibowitz, the brilliant lawyer, had the prosecution on the defensive right from the start. He managed to convince the jury that Coll was actually being framed by the police, the District Attorney and the powerful organised crime figures whom had been deeply embarrassed by the Irishman's activities. Coll, the alleged child killer, was portrayed as the victim.

When it turned out that the chief prosecution witness was a serial perjurer who virtually made a living from giving evidence on behalf of the police, and had lied about it on the stand, the trial effectively collapsed. Assistant District Attorney James T. Neary, the chief prosecutor, was forced to make a motion that the charges by dismissed and Judge Joseph E. Corrigan complied. Coll walked out of court a free man on 28 December.

There were also dark rumours about witnesses and jury members being either intimidated or bought off, a not unusual practice at the time in the murky world of the New York criminal justice system. Many policemen and politicians were in the direct pay of the gangsters made immensely rich by prohibition. In 1929, New York Police Commissioner Grover Whalen was paid $35,000 a month by the infamous crime figure Arnold Rothstein, the man who fixed the 1919 Baseball World Series.

So Coll was a free man, but he must have known his days were numbered. He tried to go back to his old rackets, but there was a small army of hitmen on his trail. On 1 February 1932, a team of gunmen burst into an apartment where Coll was said to be staying and killed two of his associates and a woman who happened to be there. Coll himself turned up at the apartment just thirty minutes after the shooting. Seven days later, Coll was in a phone-booth in a drug-store on 23rd Street at 12.30am when a car drew up outside and one man walked in. Carrying a machine gun, he whispered to the clerk behind the counter, 'Keep cool, now', and opened fire on the glass booth. Some fifteen bullets were taken out of Coll's body later on at the morgue. He was twenty-three years old. Coll was said to have been on the phone to Owney Madden at the time, threatening to kill him if he didn't hand over a pile of money.

One of the only witnesses to the hit was, by coincidence, a Donegal-born woman called Peggy Bonner who had been working at a nearby hotel where Vincent was said to be hiding out.

Coll's killer was never caught, but the gangland rumour was that the hit had been ordered by his old boss Dutch Schultz and carried out by one of Vincent's former associates, who went under the name Fats McCarthy. Vincent did leave a wife behind him, a shady woman called Lottie Kreisberger-Coll, herself a killer, serial bigamist and gangster's moll. Lottie was jailed for her part in a gangland murder two years later. She served her time and disappeared after her release from prison.

Vincent was buried in St Raymond's cemetery in the Bronx, close to his brother Peter.

There were few mourners at the funeral. His family were all dead, his former associates happy to see the back of him. There was one letter of condolence, from Alice Diamond, the widow of his former criminal associate Legs.

In the downtime between his various criminal acts, Coll was said to have talked about someday retiring home to Donegal with his loot, leaving the mean streets of New York far behind him. But few gangsters of the era ever got close to retirement age. And Vincent Coll, for all his mad bravado, must have known that he would never enjoy a peaceful old age.

SOURCES

1. 'James 'Sligo' Jameson, The Whiskey Cannibal and the Heart of Darkness'

Boylan, Henry, Ed., *A Dictionary of Irish Biography*, (Gill & Macmillan, 1998)

Jameson, Mrs James S. , Ed., *The Story Of The Rear Column Of The Emin Pasha Relief Expedition – By The Late James S. Jameson*, (London & New York, 1891)

Liebowitz, Daniel & Pearson, Charles, *The Last Expedition – Stanley's Mad Journey Through The Congo*, (W.W. Norton & Co, 2005)

Stanley, Henry Morton, *In Darkest Africa*, (1890)

Burke's Irish Family Records

Oxford Dictionary of National Biography

The New York Times

The Times of London

2. 'Antoine Walsh, Amazing Grace and the Irish Slavers of East Africa'

Klein, Herbert S., *The Atlantic Slave Trade* (Cambridge, 1999)

Rodgers, N., 'The Irish and The Atlantic Slave', *History Ireland* (May 2007)

Thomas, Hugh, *The Slave Trade* (Simon & Schuster, 1997)

The W.E.B. Du Bois database of slaving voyages

The archives of the Comtes de Serrant.

3. 'Luke Ryan, Benjamin Franklin's Irish Pirate'

Coyle, Eugene, 'An Irish Buccaneer', *History Ireland Magazine*, Summer 1999

Morley, Vincent, *Irish Opinion and the American Revolution, 1760-1783*, (Cambridge University Press, 2002)

Shiels, J., 'Captain Luke Ryan of Rush', *Dublin Historical Record* (1971)

The Freeman's Journal (Dublin, 1779)

The Gentleman's Magazine (June, 1789)

Hibernian Magazine (May, 1782)

4. 'Colonel William Cotter – And The Munster Farmers Who Fought The

Emperor Of Brazil'

Barman, Roderick J., *Citizen Emperor: Pedro II and the Making of Brazil, 1825–1891* (Stanford University Press, 1999)

Lloyd Hodges, Col G., *Narrative of the Expedition to Portugal in 1832* (James Fraser, Regent Street, London, 1833)

McCauley, Neil, *Dom Pedro, The Struggle For Liberty in Brazil and Portugal, 1798-1834* (Duke University Press)

Murray, Edmundo, 'William Cotter, Irish officer in Dom Pedro's army of imperial Brazil', *Irish Migration Studies in Latin America* Vol. 4, No. 3: July 2006

Sullivan, Dr Eileen A., 'Irish mercenaries in nineteenth-century Brazil' (Director, the Irish Educational Association, Inc., Gainesville, FL, 2005)

Walsh, The Reverend Robert C.E., *Notices of Brazil in 1828 and 1829* (London: Frederick Westley & A.H. Davis, 1830)

The Admiral Brown Society. Foxford, Co. Mayo.

5. 'Sir Hugh Gough – Limerick's Opium Warlord'

Chang Hsin-pao, *Commissioner Lin and the Opium War* (Harvard University Press, 1964)

Greenberg, M., *British Trade and the Opening of China, 1800-1842* (Cambridge University Press, 1951)

Rait, Robert S., *The Life and Campaigns of Hugh, First Viscount Gough, Field-Marshal* (London, 1903)

Waley, A., *The Opium War through Chinese Eyes* (George Allen and Unwin, 1958)

6. 'Alejandro 'Bloody' O'Reilly – Despot, Executioner, Meath Man'

Dalrymple, William, *Travels Through Spain And Portugal* (London, 1777)

Hull, Anthony H., *Charles III and The Revival of Spain* (University Press of America, 1980)

Montero de Pedro, José, *The Spanish in New Orleans and Louisiana* (Pelican Publishing Company Inc, 2000)

The Collected Letters of Jane Carlyle (Duke University, 1952)

'The Irish Presence in Cuba', www.irlandeses.org

London Review Magazine, Vol 6 1776

7. 'Beauchamp Bagenal & The Gentlemanly Art of Legalised Murder'

Atkinson, John A., *British Duelling Pistols*

Barrington, Jonah, *Personal Sketches of His Own Times*, 3 Vols (London, 1827–1832)

Melville, Lewis, *Famous Duels and Assassinations* (Gale Research Co., 1974)

O'Ferrall, F., *Daniel O'Connell* (Dublin, 1981)

Leinster Journal, July 1768

8. 'O'Dwyer and Dyer – the Butchers of Amritsar'

Dav College for Women, *Amritsar; Operation Blue Star, Jallianwala Bagh Massacre* (Amritsar. LLC Books, 2010)

Draper, Alfred, *Amritsar: The Massacre That Ended The Raj* (Cassell, 1981)

Lapping, Brian, *End of Empire* (1985)

O'Dwyer, Michael, *India As I Knew It* (1925)

Time (March, 1942)

9. 'Malachi Martin – Godfather of the American Chain-Gang'

Fryman, Mildred L., 'Career of a "Carpetbagger": Malachi Martin in Florida', *The Florida Historical Quarterly*, January 1978

Mancini, Matthew J., *One Dies, Get Another; Convict Leasing In The American South 1866-1928* (University of Southern Carolina Press, 1996)

Powell, J.C., *American Siberia* (Chicago, 1891)

Civil War Letters of Thomas Francis Meagher.

10. 'Burke & Hare – The Resurrection Men'

Hugh, Douglas, *Burke and Hare*, Douglas Hugh (Hale, 1973)

Ross, Ian, 'Body snatching in Nineteenth-Century Britain', *British Journal of Law and Society*, 6: 108–118 (1976)

Blackwood's Magazine (Edinburgh, 1829)

Newry Telegraph, 1829

Surgeon's Hall Museum, Edinburgh.

The Times of London, February 1829

'Burke and Hare', *Notable British Trials,* (Wm Hodge & Co, Edinburgh, 1921)

11. *'Vincent Mad Dog Coll, Original Gaeilgeoir Gangster, Mob Hitman and Child-Killer'*

Downey, Patrick, *Gangster City: The History of The New York Underworld 1900-1935* (Barricade Books, NJ 2004)

Horan, James David, *The Desperate Years: A Pictorial History of The Thirties,* (Crown, New York, 1962)

Tyler, Gus, *Organised Crime In America,* (University of Michigan Press, 1967)

New York Times, October 1931, February 1932.